Life Adds Up

in

Numberland the Musical

By

Auriel Wyndham Livezey

Mountaintop Publishing

If thou of fortune be bereft,
and in thy store there be but left
two loaves, sell one, and with the
dole, buy hyacinths to feed thy soul

John Greenleaf Whittier

Dedication

For my beloved mother

Rosalind L. Wyndham

who would often quote the words,
"buy hyacinths to feed thy soul"
for she believed it was just
as important to feed the soul
as the body

Table of Contents

Act 1

Act 11

Life Adds Up in Numberland the Musical

By Auriel Wyndham Livezey

This is both a workshop and a musical play

The History of Numberland

- *Numberland* was first published as a book in 1995, and was later adapted into a musical play by the author, who wrote the play, lyrics and composed the music.

- The two music CDs are enjoyed by children and adults alike. *Numberland Songs* contains all the music from the play, and *Numberland* contains a good portion of the music but also dialogue.

- The play was chosen, in short form, by Borders' Books in Long Beach, CA. as their contribution to Art Appreciation Month, October of 1998.

- The play was only briefly performed as a whole in 2005, but received wonderful reviews from audience and players alike.

Life Adds Up in Numberland the Musical

is being published with a dual purpose

Firstly, with quotations from thinkers across the ages, this script would be an excellent vehicle for individuals, discussion groups, book clubs and for churches in considering life's larger meaning and the issues surrounding us. Secondly, it still has the possibility of being mounted as a play.

About the *Numberland Songs CD:*
It is not absolutely necessary to include this in the workshop, though it would increase the enjoyment of it. The lyrics are embedded in bold throughout the script, and they will shed further light on the character who is singing.

Credit is given to Wikipedia for much of the information regarding the authors whose quotations introduce each scene.

This workshop and play are for you if:

You've ever had a problem with being labeled or bullied.

You've wanted to be a "perfect 10" or had body-image issues.

You've had concerns about your resources.

You've had questions about death.

You've experienced or contemplated the color or race question.

You've wondered about your individual worth.

You've ever felt you were being mentally manipulated.

You've experienced incompatibility with members of the opposite sex.

You've wondered about the highest form of love.

Those nine questions are the headlines or topics for each scene. How the players handle their problems can be instructive for our own lives. That these life lessons take the form of an allegory is of great advantage. Why?

Firstly, because such a format draws less criticism of ideals. Our play must go on unhampered by the brutal battery of public opinion.

Secondly, you may enter at any level you choose, and you may change your level at any time. The three levels are:

1. The play's basic level of enjoyment.

2. The moral level of how we treat others and ourselves.

3. The spiritual level of higher and better ideals.

With that wide-open field of interpretation available, there's only one more thing to say. Do enjoy this tale of human nature as it searches for a. . .

North Star, a perfect principle to life,

and for that better self

we know to be present and available to us all!

Brief Overview

Turnover Tech is a special school that accepts students of various ages and interests with the aim of helping them learn life through the subjects they take. The pilot math class turns into an adventure after students identify with numbers and arrive in Chalkland as three-dimensional chalk numbers.

There they must solve the greatest problem of all—who they really are in Numberland. The odd numbers are male and the evens are female.

After learning many lessons, at the play's finale, the students transition back to their class with a changed outlook and aim in life.

* * * * * * *

Each scene of the play is introduced by quotations from modern and ancient thinkers, that help set the stage for the scene. For instance, the following quotation by Suzy Kassem introduces Scene 1 of Act 1, where Number 10 visits Number 1 to discuss the envy being heaped on her due to her chalk "perfection."

**In a superficial world, body image is everything.
But in a world filled with substance, a beautiful mind,
heart and soul are everything.**

That statement is the perfect keynote to this play, in which the characters need to work at exchanging the superficial, temporary world of Chalkland for the world filled with real substance, which is represented by Numberland.

Cast of characters

Number 1	Glen Goodman	Teacher
Number 911	Andy Able	Campus Emergencies

Students:

Number 411	NED	Nerd as Narrator
Number 10	ANGELA	The beauty queen
Number 39	T.D.	Football hero
Number 100	SERENA	Student teacher
Number 5	FREDDIE	Unimportant kid
Number 33112	BELLA	Uncertain of herself
Number 9	MIKE	The news reporter
Number 342	BONNIE	The business woman
Number 531	PREZ	The politician
Number 532	KITTY	The loyal fan
Percent sign	LITTLE HELPER	Quiet girl

Pronunciation: 911 (nine-one-one), 411 (four-one-one), 39 (thirty-nine), 100 (one hundred), 33112 (three, three, one, one, two), 342 (three forty-two), except when speaking of an amount. 531(five thirty-one), 532 (five thirty-two).

Cast composition:

Cast of thirteen: two more mature male actors (for Number 1 and 911) and two young adolescents (one male for 5 and one female for percent sign). The remaining nine could be of any age; teens, young adults or even a senior or two, as the ages vary at Turnover Tech. Most parts do not require strong vocal abilities as much of it is character singing. Number 1 and Number 10 should have strong singing talent and good comedic ability.

NOTE: Odd numbers are male, even are female., They should be dressed distinctly differently. Little Helper (Gus) is in overalls, but in last scene of the play she is in a dress. Also each number is totally in one color and many colors represented. Color is according to dress not skin. Please refer to color songs and suggested color list on page 117. Characters are dressed according to their hopes and aspirations. For instance, in Chalkland Number 10 has a crown and a sash with "perfect 10" across it. Later in play this is simply "10."

Special note for large companies of players:

Simple ways of adding cast: for instance, adding to classroom size and also for dance scenes. This script was kept to a minimum of players for small companies and to accommodate smaller stages, but it is simple to upgrade the size of the cast for a larger production.

The unexamined life is not worth living.

Socrates (469-399 B.C.) is at once the most exemplary and the strangest of the Greek philosophers. He grew up during the golden age of Pericles' Athens, served with distinction as a soldier, but became best known as a questioner of everything and everyone. His style of teaching—immortalized as the Socratic Method—involved not conveying knowledge but rather asking question after clarifying question until his students arrived at their own understanding.

The function of education is to teach one to think intensively and to think critically. Intelligence plus character - that is the goal of true education.

Martin Luther King Jr. (1929 – 1968) was an African-American Baptist minister and activist who was a leader in the Civil Rights Movement. Known for his role in civil rights using nonviolent civil disobedience based on his Christian beliefs. He helped organize the 1963 March on Washington. In 1964, King received the Nobel Peace Prize for combating racial inequality through nonviolent resistance.

This preplay scene gives us the opportunity to examine the characters, ourselves and the human tendency to label others

Through pride we are ever deceiving ourselves. But deep down below the surface of the average conscience a still, small voice says to us, something is out of tune.

Carl Gustav Jung (1875 - 1961) was a Swiss psychiatrist and psychoanalyst who founded analytical psychology. His work has been influential in psychiatry, anthropology, archaeology, literature, religious studies. He collaborated for some time with Sigmund Freud, but later broke with him. Jung is best known for concepts such as, the collective unconscious, extroversion and introversion.

This above all: To thine own self be true; And it must follow, as the night day, Thou canst not then be false to any man.

William Shakespeare (1564 – 1616) was an English poet, playwright, and actor, who was widely regarded as the greatest writer in the English language and the world's pre-eminent dramatist. His numerous plays have been translated into every major living language and are performed more often than those of any other playwright. The quotation above is from *Hamlet*.

Life Adds Up in Numberland the Musical

By Auriel Wyndham Livezey

Preplay Scene

School buzzer goes off and a rowdy group enters the classroom with all students present except Freddie. Chairs for pupils. The teacher is presiding at a lectern. A large cardboard percent sign and some geometry symbols such as angles are tacked to wall, and large initials T.T. for Turnover Tech.

TEACHER

Good afternoon, Class.

SERENA

Good afternoon, Mr. Goodman.

Class keeps talking. Teacher looks at paper handed him by Freddie who has just entered, and motions him to a seat. Teacher raps on his lectern.

TEACHER

Your attention please! As you know,
Turnover Tech helps students learn life
no matter what class they take. So,
from now on, you'll find quotations from
ancient and modern thinkers in your
workbooks. Some of them were and are
masters in communication.

KITTY

How come? The ancients didn't even have
cell phones, did they?

1

No, Kitty, they didn't, and that was
probably a plus for them, not a minus.

Prez points at Freddie

PREZ

What's he doing here? He's just a kid! He
can't even vote yet.

TEACHER

Not everything revolves around your
political ambitions, Prez. And you should
know by now that this school accepts
students of various ages. So, let's all
welcome Freddie.

Half-hearted applause. Then he speaks to Freddie.

>   TEACHER
> Freddie, this class is a pilot program,
> aimed at helping you learn life through
> mathematics. It may get deep into
> math, but don't worry. We'll have many
> resources available to help you.

>   T.D.
> Say, teach, <u>I'm</u> not a bit worried. I've got
> a big career ahead of me... big bucks...
> loads of resources. That's the name of the
> game.

He twirls his football in the air.

>   TEACHER
> T.D. you wouldn't recognize a real
> resource if it tackled you. And by the
> way, the game of life, like mathematics,
> needs a principle to operate by, and I can
> tell you right now... it's not big bucks.
> And my name is not "teach." In fact, <u>you</u>
> may call me "Sir."

>   T.D.
> Yes, Sir! I don't want to be sent to the
> principal's office. Ooh.

>   PREZ
> Why not, T.D.! You used to spend a lot
> of time there. Besides Turnover Tech
> doesn't have a principal, remember?

T.D. glares at Prez

>   TEACHER
> That's enough. You're all here for your
> own particular needs. So, let's go over
> some points. Please stand up as I call
> your name. Bella, you need to subtract
> uncertainty, and add a little confidence.
> T.D. and Mike, you both need to multiply
> the wonderful asset of self-control.

He pauses. Bella hangs her head as she stands up, while Mike and T.D.
nudge each other and smile. They all sit again.

TEACHER

And Bonnie Billing. Hmm, you'd be a
good business executive but you get so
nitty gritty. Three hundred and forty-two
points on your business plan? Way too
much detail.

Bonnie looks disgusted, grumbles and sits down again.

BONNIE B.

But I like detail!

TEACHER

And Ned, you seem totally lost in your
computer and a multitude of facts. Maybe
you ought to begin deleting some of them.

NED

But I think they're all important. It's
hard to pare down.

TEACHER

Think again, Ned! And Prez, you and
Kitty need to concentrate more on your
studies than getting you elected campus
president. Now Angela, if you'd save your
grooming rituals for later, you might be
able to learn something. You can't depend
on beauty pagents forever.

They each stand and sit down. Angela puts her mirror in her purse.

TEACHER

Serena, I see you need extra math to
teach in the student learning lab. You're
usually cheerful if you don't get too
intense over what you do. Your test scores
were mostly 100%, weren't they?

She stands and nods then sits again.

T.D.

And Miss 100% always makes everyone
look so good, huh! She's the kind that'll
get you kicked off the football team.

Class makes consoling noises and noise in general.

TEACHER

Hey, you need to take this seriously.
Math teaches us great lessons about life.
Everyone needs to do well at math.

KITTY

But it's so hard. I just don't have a head
for numbers.

MIKE

Say T.D. She gives "airhead" new
meaning, huh?!

They chuckle.

TEACHER

A little courtesy would be welcome. Kitty,
if you identify with the numbers, that
could help. In fact, you should all try it
and you might discover a whole new world
called Numberland. But to get there you
have to be true to yourselves.

KITTY

What does that mean, Mr. Goodman?

TEACHER

Don't kid yourself about your own
motives. Be honest with yourself, and
then you'll be honest with others too.

KITTY

That sounds hard. Does that mean we
have to admit stuff to ourselves about
ourselves?

TEACHER

Yes, it does. And you can't accept labels
you put on yourself or that other people
put on you. That's not being fair or true
to yourself, your better self. Think about
that. Now, remember, today is exploration
day. I expect you to come up with some
new math ideas on learning life.

A knock on the door. Andy Able pokes his head in then enters with a young
girl.

TEACHER

Come on in, Mr. Able. Oh, you have your
little your niece with you today. I bet
she'helps a lot. Does she like doing math?

MR. ABLE

Oh, she does. She's especially good at
percentages. Yes, Gus is a great help,
that's for sure. That's why I call her
"Little Helper."

TEACHER

We could use her in this class. But, what's going on? Lots of work as usual?

MR. ABLE

Yup. All kinds of emergency campus calls. I have to wear so many hats. We've had trouble with the lights and now the computers are down. I'll need to work on the main frame in the control center. Is that okay?

TEACHER

Of course, but we're doing some science experiments out there. Stay away from the converter field. Hey, hold on a minute. Maybe I'd better go with you. Serena, would you take over please?

SERENA

Oh, sure!

TEACHER

Here's a tip for today's lesson. You're all like actors. You each have an important part to play in life with *no understudy*. Give Freddie an idea of the class, and when you come up with a plan of action, you can leave for the day.

He, Able and little helper exit and class begins talking loudly. Serena sits in front.

SERENA

Does anyone have a comment on this class for Freddie? How about you, Bella?

BELLA

No, not me! I don't have anything worthwhile to say. I never do.

ANGELA

Well, I want to make a comment. I'm not sure I like being in a mixed group like this! Won't help my social standing on campus.

FREDDIE

Your standing! I don't even have one. No one thinks I'm the least bit important. It just gets to me.

NED
Freddie, the basic thing in this class is to memorize math facts, the more facts the better.

T.D.
That's not it. Don't think about anything. Just dive in and tackle it!

FREDDIE
How do we do that?

SERENA
Well, Mr. Goodman said to identify with the numbers. That could help. Maybe we could all have a number.

PREZ
Does he think we're little kids? This sounds really juvenile. But it might suit you, Freddie.

T.D. to Serena

T.D.
We know what number you'd be Miss Average Raiser. You'd be Number 100.

MIKE
Hey T.D. That could be useful to us. Say, Serena, why exactly do you want to be a teacher?

SERENA
Well, I like to help people learn. I just like to help.

MIKE
See T.D. She can do our assignments and we'll all be happy. She wants to help and we'll get 100 percent. It's a win-win situation.

T.D.
Riiiight!

ANGELA
I rather like this game. It suits me. I think the girls should be even numbers because all you guys are so odd!

NED
But I don't want people to think I'm odd.

ANGELA

They already do. Get over it! Now, let's see, what number would I be? Oh, a perfect 10, of course!

Mike agrees sarcastically and then points to Prez

MIKE

Of course! And our wanna-be campus president is always trying to get votes. Posters everywhere saying, "call me at extension 531." So that's what he'd be... Number 531.

T.D.

And Kitty always follows him around so she'd be....

T.D. and MIKE together

532! Yeah!

They laugh and hi-five each other.

BONNIE

Think you're so smart don't you Mr. Low Grades and what number would you be?

T.D.

Well, Miss 342 point business plan, just one look at my football jersey ought'a tell ya. I'm Number 39.

FREDDIE

What about me? What about me? Don't I get a number?

PREZ

Oh yes, but it should be something suitable for you like my number is for me. Let's see, a number for someone who doesn't quite fit in. Hmm, when things don't add up, it's like saying 2 and 2 are 5. Yes, that's what you can be, Number 5.

FREDDIE

That's not nice. That's not fair, is it? Say something, Ned!

T.D.

Yes, just what does Ned the Nerd have to say? Lost all the facts running around in your computer head?

NED

No, as a matter of fact I haven't. It's just
useless to waste my breath on things
that have no purpose. And being nasty is
purposeless. It's like having a colorless
character.

MIKE

Hey, how 'bout that? Yep, a number
with color. I should have a classy color...
like grey, 'cause I'll be reporting on the 9
o'clock news one of these days.

BONNIE

And how, Mr. 9 o'clock, do you know what
the color of a number is? There's a real
number behind the chalk number.

MIKE

Don't worry your poor little head about it.
Color of chalk is good enough.

NED

If you're going to be a chalk number, not a
real number, then I could just erase you.

T.D.

Don't get technical on us. We don't care
about small details like that. We only
care about big ones like the size of your
shoes Bella. Your name should be grander
than just Bella. How about Bellagrande?

NED

Don't you know it's the sign of a small
character to make fun of people's names?
That's how they identify themselves.

T.D.

One more fact out of you Mr. Computer
Head, and we'll make you the number
in charge of all the facts! Oh, poor Bella
looks so blue. Don't worry, Bella. We'll
give you a number. How about 33112?

BELLA

But that's so big. Everyone else has much
smaller, cuter numbers.

MIKE

Well, if the shoe fits, wear it. That's what
they say.

ANGELA

You're both so cruel. Not everyone can
be perfectly proportioned like me. But
speaking of color, I'd be a striking red
don't you think, not a shrinking violet like
Kitty. (motions to Kitty and adds) Oh,
nothing personal.

NED

And what are all these colored chalk
numbers doing? Are they just running
around on the Chalkboard?

T.D.

I dunno. If we're supposed to be like
actors then maybe the numbers are
putting on a play. Who knows, who
cares?

KITTY

But how does it help to identify with
numbers? What's our plan of action?

T.D.

Hey, guys! Let's follow Mr. Goodman to
the control center. We can explore it and
maybe we'll even discover Numberland.

ANGELA

Oh, a field trip. I just love trips.

NED

But it's off campus and hard to find. Does
anyone know the way?

MIKE

We'll figure it out.

T.D.

Say, we could take the small school bus.
I've got a deck of cards. The one who
draws the highest card drives us to the
land of numbers.

KITTY

But Numberland isn't really a place, is it?
Is it?

She calls this after them as they all get up to leave.

Introductions from the Preplay Scene

Make a list of the characters and what you notice most about them.

Add any comments or insights you would like to make about them.

Discussion points

Which characters interest you the most and why?

What are their pluses or minuses?

Do you identify with any of these characters and why?

Do you feel there is a "better you" waiting to be revealed or lived? What do you think it would be like?

Do you have people in your life that are like any of the characters?

Today, many people consider situations and people they encounter to be life lessons in this one big schoolroom called Earth. Do you feel that way too? If "no" what do you feel is our purpose here?

All the world's a stage,
And all the men and women merely players.

Shakespeare has been called "The Bard of Avon." He was a poet, playwright and actor. In addition to his 38 plays, he wrote 154 sonnets and two long narrative poems. This quotation is from his play, *As you Like It*.

When dealing with people, remember you are not
dealing with creatures of logic, but with creatures
bristling with prejudice and motivated by pride and vanity.

Dale Carnegie (1888-1955) was an American writer and lecturer and the developer of well-known courses in self-improvement, salesmanship, corporate training, public speaking, and interpersonal skills. He is well known for the book, How to Win Friends and Influence People, which was a best seller in his time, and is still very popular today.

Scene 1 encourages us to play
our part on the world stage and shows
the shallowness of body-image thinking

In a superficial world, body image is everything.
But in a world filled with substance, a beautiful mind,
heart and soul are everything.

Suzy Kassem (born 1975) is an American author, film director, philosopher, short story writer, essayist, and poet. She is of Egyptian descent and studied business, film making, and creative writing at the University of Toledo and Harvard. Her first book, *Rise up and Salute the Sun* brought a cult following of her work.

Give me beauty in the inward soul;
may the outward and the inward man be at one.

Socrates (470/469 – 399 BC) a classical Greek (Athenian) philosopher wrote nothing himself, so all that is known about him is filtered through the writings of a few contemporaries and followers, most of all, his student Plato. He was accused of corrupting the youth of Athens and sentenced to death. Choosing not to flee, he spent his final days in the company of his friends before drinking the executioner's cup of poisonous hemlock.

Life Adds Up in Numberland the Musical

ACT 1

Scene 1

Medley played of Numberland songs. Voices can be heard calling out from backstage, "Where are we?" "Why does that sign say "Chalkland?" "Who was driving the bus?"

PRELUDE track, number 1 is played.
Characters for this scene are Numbers 411,10, 9, 5, 39, 342, 33112, 1, 100, percent sign (small girl).   Costumes are according to characters own view of themselves.

Costume change during Prelude. Numbers drift across stage. E.g. 342 with briefcase looks impatiently at her watch and refuses to be interviewed by 9 with a mike. 5 hugs pinata in shape of a 5. Number 39 twirls his football.   10 meanders and stares at herself in a mirror, patting her hair. 532 waves flags behind 531 as he crosses stage.

Large percent sign and geometry symbols are still on wall, also initials T.T. There is a hat-tree marked "911's hats" (see prop list) which remains on stage. 411 enters at end of Prelude to center stage as they have all left.

411
Welcome. I'm Number 411, the number
with all the information. That's why
I've been called to introduce this play,
Numberland, which, however, takes
place in Chalkland, where everything,
including the inhabitants, is made of
chalk. Now, the numbers who live here
on the Chalkboard really don't know what
life is all about. I mean, give them 2 and
2 and they'll make it ...5. That's just how
Chalkland is. Now, I umm...huh?

Number 5 enters bouncing a ball. Good to have 411 tall and 5 quite short and cute. 5 dribbles ball all around Number 411 who stares at him.

1
What are you doing here, Number 5?

5
I heard my number. Is this my cue?

411
No, it's not your cue. I'm setting the stage
for the audience.

5
But the stage is already set.

                    411
I know the stage is already set. I'm here
to give them the facts.

                    5
You're giving them the fax, the facsimile,
and not the real thing?

                    411
Really, 5! The facts not the fax. But now
that you've brought it up, everything in
Chalkland is a facsimile and not the real
thing. And ... something was lost in the
transmission.

Looks meaningfully at 5, and then 5 looks himself over.

                    5
It was?

                    411
It was. That's why we have to understand
Numberland, the real world of numbers.
Now, please go away and wait for your
wake-up call.

                    5
Oh, alright, if you promise not to call any
more wrong numbers, like 5, when you
really don't mean it at all.

5 grumbles, as he sits near plants which 10 will pour water onto. 411 sighs.

                    411
Our Chalkland numbers don't know it
yet but they're going to have to solve the
greatest problem of all—what and who
they really are in Numberland. Now, I
invite you to join the numbers as they
travel into... inner space.

"Perfect 10's perfect patio" sign stuck into a plant with a couple more plants
beside it. 10 enters, picks up watering can and waters the plants. She hums
her song and looks at herself in the mirror in her other hand while she pours
water across plants onto 5 sitting below. Then 10 goes to center stage and 5
slowly follows her, brushing himself off. He is supposed to be quite wet.

                    10
Aah. Another good day in Chalkland; a
little less chalkdust in the air than usual.
She sees 5 who is brushing the water off.

10

Oh, hello Number 5, have you been
swimming again? You shouldn't stay too
long in the water. It makes little chalk
bodies all puckery.

5

No, Number 10, I was waiting for my
cue...you know, my wake-up call.

10

You're alert, that's good. Take me, I
notice everything.

5

Right!

He brushes off more water.

10

For instance, I know numbers ask a lot
of questions about me, so I'm composing
a musical answer. Maybe you could find
some numbers who'd like to take part.
Oh, uh...strictly background work, of
course.

5

Oh okay, background work.

He runs offstage

10

Now, let's see, I can just imagine there's
an audience here with all those questions.

10 curtsies to her imaginary audience then sings"

"A NUMBER SO PERFECT AS I"

Why do all love her, you ask each other,
Why is she so heavenly?
How come she's perfect, oh so perfect?
Well,
It's you see 'cause I'm just me.
After all...

What can be done to better me?
Does the law of perfection apply?
What can be done to better me?
A number so perfect as I.

Number 39 walks by behind her during this next verse , pauses to listen, laughs, mimics her by putting hand on hip to simulate a fashion model.

How can more beauty be given me?
New descriptions I simply defy. (Holds up a mirror and peers in it).
How can more beauty be given me?
A number so lovely as I.

Number 39 walks off stage laughing just before verse ends. 342, 33112, 9, and 5 enter behind 10 holding placards with <u>question marks</u> on them. They come out singing the bridge, 10 glances behind her motioning to them to hurry.

Background singers
You had questions, endless questions,
It's just fair that she can share
All the answers to your questions,

10 sings last line of bridge
Then you'll see why you love me.

Then background singers say
For instance

10 resumes singing.
What more light can be shone on me?
As an answer I hear a big sigh. (Cups hand to ear to listen.)
What more light can be shone on me?
A number so brilliant as I.

Optional: During that third verse a number 39 could shine a spotlight or flashlight on various parts of stage while 10 tries to follow it. It ends up highlighting trash basket beside her.

How could you be more proud of me?
I know you'll just simply deny. (Giggles and waves a finger at audience).
How could you be more proud of me?
A number so humble as I.

At last line, background singers turn placards,<u> one at a time,</u> with number 10 written on other side. Number 9 has 9.9 on his, and turns it to coincide with last word of song. Evens leave and odds talk behind 10. She glances back at sign and hears them.

5
Number 9 , why'd you do that?

9
Just making a statement. Numbers are
always try to fractionalize me, push me
up to 9.9. Huh! Just an attempt to get
me closer to 10, I'm sure, and as though I
wanted to be a perfect 10 anyway!

Mumbles as they exit.

10

Nonsense! All numbers want to be like
me. That's plain old envy. Well, I'm
going to talk to Number 1 about this even
if I have to visit his classroom to do it.

10's patio is removed and she exits passing 100, who enters with percent
sign by the hand. 100 crosses to other side of stage, where Number 1 has just
entered. 100 looks burdened.

100

Oh, Number 1, could I talk to you for a minute?

1

Of course, Number 100. Say, how do you
like student teaching?

100

Oh, I do enjoy it. I'm teaching basic math
right now. Maybe later I'll get to teach
harmony or geometry. But... I've been
told I can't until I solve my problem.

1

What's that?

100

Well, it's my nature to be tickled pink but
instead I feel so burdened, so responsible
for other numbers. I try to take the
percent sign with me everywhere I go, so
I'm always ready to help.

Holds up her hand that is holding the hand of the percent sign.

1

Oh I see, you want the students to be
happy and successful 100 percent of the
time. But you need to show them how to
work out their own problems. You can't
do it all for them.

100

I know it doesn't help students to let them
lean on me.

She sighs and hangs her head.

1

Exactly! They need to understand and apply math rules. Then they can lean on the Principle of Mathematics and not on you. But your situation isn't unusual. In fact, I've had to learn that lesson more than once.

100

But you're a teacher. You surely know it all.

1

Oh, no. Any good teacher is always learning too. Listen to how I figured out this problem.

He motions her to sit, and percent can sit or stand, and then 1 sings.

"LET GO OF YOUR BURDEN"

I wondered as I walked along
When I would be set free.
I waited for the day to come
When joy would walk with me.
Till I leaned on our Principle
Which made us to be free
And as I walked each day with joy
Then joy did walk with me.
This truth you too shall see.

Let go of your burden
Let go of your care,
Let go of your burden
It's not yours to bear,
Our Principle tells us
So tenderly,
Let go of your burden
And come lean on me.

If able to do this
A bright light we'll be
Then others will find that
They too can be free.
It's not up to you
It's not up to me
A higher law governs
With love you see.
It's so good to let go of sorrow
We can learn to live without fear
You don't have to wait for tomorrow
You will find that joy is here.

So, come out of the darkness
To where it's all bright,
Come out of the shadows
And into the light.
We're in this together
We're one family
Let go of your burden
Or share it with me.

Let go of your burden
Or share it with me.

Number 1 takes the hand of the percent sign at this point.

100

Oh, Number 1, that's so encouraging. I
really want to strike the right balance of
when to help.

1

Then remember, some numbers do too
little for others, and some do too much, so
listen for the answer. Every problem has
a solution.

100

Thank you Number 1. And I'll listen.

They exit stage left, while 5 enters from stage right bouncing his ball with 10
offstage, calling him. She arrives on stage too.

10

Number 5! Number 5! I'd like you to run
an errand for me.

5

Is it something important?

10

Everything I do is important. Now, I
want you to tell Number 1 that I'll be
coming to see him in a few minutes. Just
prepare him for my visit. Hmm, you
know, there's something cute about you,
something that reminds me ...of me.

100 re-enters from stage left with percent sign, no longer holding its hand.
They walk behind and pause between 5 and 10.

5

Ooh. You've got the percent sign, Number
100. That's a good idea.

                            10
I'm not sure about that.

100 and the percent sign look back and forth at 10 and 5 as at a tennis match.

                             5
It makes you look very important.

                            10
Makes you stand out too much.

                             5
Must be good to get a lot of attention.

                            10
Must be tiring to have numbers looking
at you. Uh, Number 5, did I just hear
your number being called? It may be
important.

                             5
Oh.
He rushes offstage.
                            10
Opinions are very stimulating, don't you
agree? Especially correct opinions. Well,
it was nice having this conversation
with you but I have to get ready for an
appointment. Bye now.

10 hurries off while 100 and the percent look at each other and shrug.
Number 9 comes up with clipboard in hand, figuring things out. He hails her
with the pencil.

                             9
Oh Number 100, I've got a problem. All
this information and a weird question.
"Who was driving the bus?" What does
that mean? This is s'posed to be today's
news report, and it just doesn't add up.
Can you help?

                            100
Of course, Number 9.

She takes the pencil and clipboard and does some figuring.

                            100
Oh, there are so many minuses here your
news has ended up completely on the
negative side. We'll just correct those
errors and . . .

9 leans his elbow on 100's shoulder.

                              9
                I knew I could depend on you to do this
                for me.

The underscoring of "Let go of your burden" begins. 100 stops and looks up.

                              9
                What's the matter?

                             100
                I was just listening... uh, thinking that
                now the errors are corrected you can work
                out the rest of the problem yourself. Just
                make sure the greater percentage of the
                news is on the plus side, or... solution
                oriented.

                              9
                You think I can do it? I'll need to use the
                percent sign.

                             100
                Of course you can do it, and the percent
                sign is for all of us to use. It's very
                helpful.

The little percent sign nods its head vigorously.

                              9
                Alright. Huh! I guess I'll, uh, try that.
                Thanks, Number 100.

This is almost the end of the 50 seconds of music. 9 shows the percent sign
the figures on the clipboard and they both nod as they walk off. Underscoring
reaches the final crescendo as 100 smiles, stands erect and walks off stage. 5
runs out.

                              5
                No one was calling me, no one, as usual!

Crosses stage to see Number 1 who has just entered from other side and is
bringing out lectern and chairs.

                              1
                Ah Number 5. How are things with you?

                              5
                Not great. Chalkland's always using me
                in wrong arithmetic. Haven't you heard
                them? "That's just like saying 2 and 2 are
                5." So, I've got a question.

Why do they always use me?
It's as unfair as can be.
It could be 9
That would be fine,
Or Number 8
She's always late,
Why does it have to be me?
Why do they use me in such wrong arithmetic?
Just a good scapegoat that's me.

Why do they all pick on me,
Why won't they just let me be?
Use Number 4
Need I say more?
Or Number 3
He looks like me.
Why does it have to be me?
How can they do this without my permission
It's not very legal you see.

Why do they always choose me,
Why won't they let me be free?
We could use 6
Hey, that's a mix,
It could be you
Or Number 2,
Why does it have to be me?
My big ambition is break with tradition
And then it won't have to be me.

1
Uh-huh! So, that's your problem?

5
Yes, it is. I don't think numbers have a
very high opinion of me.

1
Oh 5, haven't you noticed how Chalkland
opinions are always changing?

5
No.

1
You will. Now, in Numberland there are
no opinions, just scientific facts like this
one. Every number has a special purpose.
Chalkland can't give you a purpose and it
can't take it away. Think about that.

5

Okay, hmm a purpose.   Oh, I was
supposed to tell you that Number 10 is
coming to see you.

1

Alright, thank you 5.

5 exits stage right and 10 enters stage left smoothing her dress and patting
her hair. She goes to Number 1, who is putting chairs in a line for his class.
She thinks he is offering her a chair.

10

Number 1? I'm Number 10 and we
met once, just briefly, but I'm sure you
remember me. Oh, thank you. (sits
down on chair) Now, you see, there's
this problem because of who I am.   Or
perhaps it's because of how I am.

1

Well, it's just . . .

10

Exactly. It's just the way the chalk was
applied to produce me, not too much or
too little.

She gets up and pats herself.

10

It's referred to as "perfectly proportioned,"
and it's become the standard for all
numbers. But, it's really impossible for
them to attain. Even I tend to fluctuate
a...

Pauses with a ldiscrete little cough.

1

Fluctuate?

10

Now, the point is, I don't mind numbers
trying to be like me, but this envy that's
always being heaped on me –such a
burden!

1

Ah, a burden.

                                    10
Right! I thought you'd understand, at
least to some degree. Many numbers may
want to be like you, Numero Uno, but just
everyone wants to be a perfect 10. There's
something so, well, perfect about it, in
every which way. (Sighs) Now there's no
one more humble than I but . . .

1 turns quickly in the other direction, laughing quietly, and 10 speaks to
herself.

                                    10
Hmm. I'm so glad Number 1 is thinking
deeply about this. Why, he's even
shaking with the effort.

Number 1 turns back to her, smiling.

                                    1
Yes, uh, I think I know what you're
saying. I've had some pretty hard lessons
to learn myself in that department.

                                    10
What do you mean hard lessons?

                                    1
Oh, it's not easy, trying to live up to what
Chalkland expects. I finally gave up
on that to learn about the real world of
numbers. Just let me tell you some of the
problems I've had with Chalkland.

                    "IT'S HARD TO BE A NUMBER 1"

It's hard to be a Number 1,
The best in all you do,
There's someone breathing down your neck
I think it's Number 2.
It's hard to be a Number 1,
You're suppos'd to look so fine,
Then who comes walking down the road
That handsome Number 9.
It's hard to be a Number 1,
It makes you feel so blue
When you're introduced to 194
And that's her IQ too.

You're supposed to reach perfection,
They expect you to go so far
And just when I think I've made it,
I look, and there you are.

She smiles and preens

10

Yes, but back to my situation. Now, this
envy thing is really not my problem, you
know; it's everyone else's. If you can't
pick up on that . . . well, maybe I have the
wrong number. What is it again that you
teach, lessons in getting to the top?

1

Oh, no. I usually teach Recognizing our
Resources. Would you like to join the new
class tomorrow?

10

Join your class? Oh, don't get me wrong.
I'm not against learning. It's just being
taught that bothers me. I'm more into
self study, particularly a study of myself.
You know, like independent study in
graduate school.

1

To me the Chalkboard is more like
preparatory school.

10

Oh, how sweet, how charming. (an aside)
And how juvenile! Well, what if I audit
your class, just to listen and not be tested
on anything, of course. Uh... tell me, is
this an exclusive school?

1

Oh, no, it doesn't exclude anyone. It's
very inclusive with numbers of all shapes
and sizes. Yes, you'd be very welcome.

10

Ooh!

Said with great disappointment and a wrinkled nose.

1

And maybe it's because of my number, but
I often get students that always want to
be first. And sometimes a timid number
that's only trying to fit in, into some space
on the Chalkboard.

                                    10
              I don't do that competitive me-first kind of
              nonsense. And as for fitting in, well, I can
              fit... into any space that accommodates
              me.

She pauses, while Number 1 is puzzled and mouths those words. 10 walks
and continues.

                                    10
              I'm not like other numbers you know.

                                    1
              Oh, I can see that.

                                    10
              Take for instance that silly duo. 532
              follows 531 everywhere while he tries to
              win the popular vote. I don't depend on
              votes for my popularity.

                                    1
              That's probably a good thing. So what
              about my class?

10 sighs deeply

                                    10
              I suppose I could make time in my day to
              audit one class, 'specially if you think it'll
              help with this envy problem.

                                    1
              Oh, it'll help. I'm sure of that.

                                    10
              I'll be on time of course. Whatever I do
              will be done perfectly.

                                    1
              We'll certainly be discussing perfection in
              this class. See you tomorrow then.

10 nods at Number 1 who is almost laughing. He exits stage left. She walks to
front of stage and meets 5 bouncing his ball coming from stage right.

                                    5
              Hello, Number 10. Did you talk to
              Number 1?

Yes, I did Number 5. Some numbers just
bounce through life on the Chalkboard,
while others have serious concerns to
attend to.

5

Are you going to take his class?

10

Yes, but only to audit. They'll be
discussing perfection and I'll probably be
used as an example.

5

Ooh.

10

And Number 1 was in such a happy mood
when I left. He was smiling, well, almost
laughing. I give such pleasure wherever
I go.

10 sings with last few notes of melody to 10's song. Waves to 5 as she exits.

10

Such pleasure wherever I go. Such
pleasure wherever I go.

She exits and 5 follows.

Discussion Points

What stood out to you the most in this scene?

Discuss the characters as they are revealed.

What life lessons can be learned from this scene?

Notes

To improve is to change; to be perfect is to change often.

Sir Winston Leonard Spencer Churchill (1874 – January 24, 1965) was a British politician and statesman, best known for his leadership of the United Kingdom during World War II. He was Prime Minister from 1940 to 1945 and from 1951 to 1955. Churchill was also an officer in the British Army, a non-academic historian, a writer and an artist. He won the Nobel Prize in Literature in 1953 for his overall, lifetime body of work. An honorary citizen of the United States.

It is not enough to be industrious; so are the ants.
What are you industrious about?

Henry David Thoreau (1817–1862) was an American essayist, poet, philosopher, abolitionist, naturalist, tax resister, development critic, surveyor, and historian. A leading transcendentalist, Thoreau is best known for his book Walden, a reflection upon simple living in natural surroundings, and his essay "Civil Disobedience," an argument for disobedience to an unjust state.

Scene 2 reveals a principle to life and discusses our most important resources

Lay not up for yourselves treasures upon earth...
But lay up for yourselves treasures in heaven.

Jesus (c.4 BC – c.AD 30/33), also referred to as Jesus of Nazareth or Christ Jesus, was a Jewish preacher and religious leader who became the central figure of Christianity. His healing works and his power over the material world have been repeated to a degree by some of his Christian followers. Jesus' impact was so great that the calendar, in most parts of the world, began again. The widely used "AD", or "CE", are based on the approximate birth date of Jesus.

The greatest legacy one can pass on to one's children and grandchildren is not money or other material things accumulated in one's life, but rather a legacy of character and faith.

William Franklin "Billy" Graham, Jr. (1918), American evangelical Christian evangelist, was ordained a Southern Baptist minister, who rose to celebrity status in 1949. Hosted the annual Billy Graham Crusades, for six decades. Spiritual adviser to American presidents; Dwight D. Eisenhower, Lyndon B. Johnson and Richard Nixon. Insisted on integration for his revivals and crusades. 1957 invited Martin Luther King, Jr. to preach jointly in New York.

ACT 1

Scene 2

Number 1's classroom, chairs center stage. Characters: 1, 10, 5, 33112, 342, 9, 39, small girl (dressed as percent sign), 531 and 532. Numbers, except for 531,532, & %, rush into class singing Rush song: a Keystone cops routine, - CD shows male and female parts. The singing begins offstage.

"RUSH SONG"

**Run, run,
Rush, rush
Run, run, run around the corner
Rush, rush, rush around the corner**

**Run, run, run around the corner
Run to Number 1's class
Rush, rush, rush around the corner
We don't want to be last!**

**Run, run, run around the corner
Run to Number 1's class
Rush, rush, rush around the corner
We don't want to be last.**

**We'll get there real fast!
We don't want to be last!**

They collide center stage near chairs at end of song. 10 is mowed down as they rush into class. They take their seats leaving 10 on the floor in front. Number 1 enters.

1
Good morning class!

He peers over his lectern at 10 sprawled on the floor in front of him.

Class
Good morning, Number 1.

Spoken like goody goodies while 10 picks herself up from the floor and flounces over to chair at the side of the stage. The percent sign, small girl, enters the room.

1
The percent sign will be with us today as
a reminder that every normal function is
available for each one of us.

The percent sign curtsies to class, which applauds, and sits on a stool to the side of the class near 10.

1

Now, let's see who are we missing?
Number 531 and 532. Oh, here they are.

531 and 532 enter. She has two small flags which she waves behind 531 as they walk in. 531 goes down the line of students with patter routines, starts with 9 and 39.

531

I'll give you the sun, I'll give you the
moon, you give me your vote, and I'll
do it real soon. (To 342 and 33112) My
standards are high, they're not that lax,
it just so happens I don't pay tax. (To 5)
I wouldn't dream of buying your vote, but
you'd look good in a brand new coat.

5

Really? (He looks pleased).

531 goes to percent sign and makes a fuss and tries to kiss it. It pushes him away. He makes a motion to 532 to cross something off the pad which she has tucked at her waist. She looks sadly at the percent sign as she does. 531 and 532 sit down. 9 Runs up to Number 1 with a mike in hand to interview him.

9

Oh, before we start and just for the
record, I have a question, Number 1.

342

Good! You're going to ask what life's all
about. What is our purpose? How did we
all get here? Important details like that.

9

No, I'm not. My question is: How come
this special school we're attending doesn't
have a principal?

5

I thought you were going to ask who was
driving the bus.

9

What are you talking Number 5! Can't
you just be quiet?

1

Number 9, all numbers have to obey the
Principle of Mathematics. Having a chalk
principal might confuse them. It just isn't
the same.

9

It isn't?

342

Of course it isn't, you chalkbrain! Have
you ever seen the Principle of numbers?
It's invisible, but it's everywhere.

9

I knew that!

1

That's a good question to introduce our
subject, Recognizing our Resources. And
just where do our resources come from?
From the Principle, with a capital P, of
numbers, the intelligence that governs
our universe. Perhaps you'd like to
expand on that, Number 342?

342

I certainly would. I just love details. Um,
Principle is the intelligence or you could
say the Mind, with a capital M, of our
universe because it has some great ideas
like numbers and their functions.

She points at percent sign. It gets off stool to curtsy. Class applauds except
for 531 who nudges 532 not to.

342

And there aren't any mistakes or errors in
the Principle of numbers, so it is the truth
too, isn't it?

1

Yes, it is. Remember, looking at
Chalkland is like looking through wavy,
clouded glass. It's not a true or accurate
view of Numberland which is perfect
without chalk limitations.

39 waves his hand.

1

What is it Number 39?

39

I understand what you're getting
at, Number 1. There are unlimited
possibilities for us. Right?

Yes, there are.

Number 39 stands up.

39
Just what I thought. But it may be more
difficult for the even numbers here to
catch on, if you know what I mean.

Chuckles, nudges 9; crosses close to 5, making a patting, smoothing motion.

9
They're usually trying to please everyone,
pat, pat, make things even. Odd numbers
know what it means to go out on the
offensive. Yes, we can be really offensive.
But...we're not insensitive to the needs of
others.

Number 5 stands.

5
Well, I have a problem. I'm always being
used in wrong ...

Number 39 pushes 5 back down in his chair.

39
Sit down, Number 5. Yes, we have
sensitivity and we do enjoy the finer
things in life, like music. Oh, wait just
a minute, a new melody is coming to me
right now.

Number 39 smirks at 10 and hums 10's tune. Da, da,, " a number so" da, da,
da. He sits down. 10 is horrified.

1
Uh yes, Number 39, most sensitive.

Number 1 pauses while 39 nods his head at others at this seeming approval
and sits down again.

1
I think it's time for an example.
Chalkland is more like Slumberland than
Numberland, so let's see if this true story
will wake you up. It's about a number
who felt he didn't add up to much in life,
so he went into the chalk mines to make
his fortune.

Number 1 sings Chalk mines song. Class interjects "why" then "Oh" at end.

"CHALK MINES"

There was a certain number, who led a minus life.
He felt so underrated, each day was full of strife.
So he made a big decision he hoped would bring him peace.
He went into the chalk mines; he took out one long lease.

He sang and worked and rolled the chalk in his money bag.
He had so much amassed he feared the bag would sag.
But he got it to the city, and with it bought much land.
He built a great estate, but... it really couldn't stand.

CLASS
Why?

1
Why?
He built beside the river edge, it began to rise.
To build so close to water, it wasn't very wise.
Though the chalk was rather sturdy it only stood one day,
And in that short amount of time, all was washed away.

(Class) OOH.

1
That number didn't get the right answer
because he depended on and invested in...
chalk. But, did you notice any pluses at
all in this equation?

9
I reported on that for the Chalkchat
News. He was a real loser!

342
That's a minus not a plus, you
chalkchatterer! I think he should have
put his problem on the office agenda. Any
point, no matter how small, deserves a
lengthy business meeting.

531
Did he analyze the statistics before going
into those Chalk mines? I depend a lot
on statistics. Put that down for my next
speech.

Turns to 532 who has a notepad. 532 nods and writes.

1

I'm not sure that he did, but that probably wouldn't have been a plus. So, Number 33112, now is the time for you to say something...anything.

33112

Well, uh... he worked hard...and he sounded honest and cheerful.

1

Aha, honesty, cheerfulness, perseverance. Yes, our real resources aren't made of chalk, so they won't wear out, wash out or fade away. Ways of doing things can change, but the true basics in life are permanent.

9

Are you saying then, Number 1, that those resources never change?

1

Yes, I am Number 9, and the fact is you can't be truly successful without them.

5

But what about numbers that are rude to other numbers?

9

Or how about dishonest numbers? Some of them look pretty successful.

9 stares at 531

531

Oh, Number 1, this would be a good time for me to get information on statistics from 411.

He gets up and so does 532

531

But I'll be joining the walk and sing harmony group later to add my special vocal talents.

532 nods and waves the flags as she follows him.

531

Call if you need. You have my number.

1

Oh, yes, I've got your number. (To the
students). Group together, please.

531 and 532 leave, students take out 2 chairs, 39, 9 and 342 will sit to right of
1 and 33112 and 5 to the left of him. 9 is standing in front with 342 and looks
back at 33112 who is dressed in blue. He holds his mike in front of 342 as
though to interview her.

9

Just for the record, Number 342.
How come your company isn't using
blue numbers? It's made them pretty
unhappy.

342

That's just their Chalkland nature. Blue
numbers are simply blue. Can't blame us
for that.

9

And what about opportunities for odd
numbers like me, or is there a ceiling on
promoting them?

342

Nonsense. Ever seen such a ceiling,
mm? Hard to prove. Anyway, your job is
incredibly easy. Why would you want one
like mine?

Lowers his mike

9

But I have to run with the news. That's
not easy.

342

Of course it is.   Most of your news runs...
downhill.

She motions downward. Then they all sit down again.

1

Class, come to order please. You were
asking about rudeness and dishonesty.
Maybe unprincipled living looks as
though it works for awhile, but . . . there's
always the day of reckoning.

A number of oh's and a chorus from the class, "the day of reckoning," followed by silence, then Number 39 raises his hand.

39

Just when is the day of reckoning,
Number 1? I want to be ready to tackle it.

1

Oh, it's anytime we have to face our own
errors. It should be every day or mistakes
just pile up. And we'll still have to correct
them.

33112

How do we do that?

1

You have to do math mentally and
accurately. We should close our eyes.

39

No surprises, right?

1

No surprises just facts. At the basis of all
correct math is a very important concept...
perfect Principle and perfect number.
But this isn't something you can just
<u>visualize</u>. It's a fact you have to <u>realize</u>.
So let's close our eyes and see how we do.

Pauses while all have eyes closed including Number 1. At this point 10 gets up and walks in front of class, but no one can see her.

1

Do you have it?

Class

I dunno. Maybe. Uh-huh. Ooooh.

She nods at them looking expectant.

1

What do you see?

5

I can't find a rude number. Where'd it go?

342

I see a happy, whole number, not
fractionalized or stressed-out.

9
And the perfect number is accurate. Huh.
No dishonesty to report on.

1
Anything else?

10 is encouraging them, her arms stretched out, expecting them to say they see her. She poses waiting.

342
Mmmm. I think this number is . . . this
perfect number is . . .an idea. Yes, an
idea, because I can't see any chalk at all.

10 throws up her hands and returns to her seat at the side, shaking her head and looking puzzled.

1
Very good. Open your eyes. You've
caught a glimpse of Numberland.
When you understand the truth about
numbers you can correct mistakes on the
Chalkboard. You'll see fractionalized
numbers become whole, crooked ones will
straighten out and fading ones will even
bounce right back again.

CLASS
Wow!

1
Now, a few minutes ago we found out
what our true resources are, but it's not
enough to recognize them, we have to use
them. So before you leave, tell us what
some of your resources are and how can
you put them into action.

Resource class song. Odds sing to each other; evens sing to each other then all sing.

"RESOURCE CLASS SONG"

Numbers take turns calling out qualities of character.

Sincerity, unselfishness, kindness, truthfulness, gentleness, goodness, purity, loyalty, peace, joy, patience, courage, love, gratitude, justice, mercy, wisdom, intelligence, integrity.

Odds stand and sing first verse

We have true strength and courage
Forbearance and patience all four.
We can get A's in humanity,
In mercy and justice galore.

Evens stand and sing

We can please our Principle
As that is the highest law,
We can please our Principle
Not fear to displease anymore.

Class stands and sings

We can express perfection
Our true nature without any flaw
We can express real goodness,
Compassion, kindness and more. Yea!

During last verse they form a line and leave; the percent sign tags along after them and curtsies to Number 1 as they exit. 10 approaches 1.

> 10
> Oh, Number 1, could I speak to you for a moment?

> 1
> Yes, 10, what is it?

> 10
> Perhaps you've noticed the glare coming in on my chair by the window, and I was just wondering, if well . . . if it would be possible for me to change that seat. I really don't mind which one, even one of those student chairs would be alright.

> 1
> Are you willing to go from auditing to being one of the pupils? Are you willing then to change your status?

> 10
> Yes ... yes, I'm willing to change. To change my status.

> 1
> Then welcome to a new world, Number 10. Welcome to Numberland.

They exit.

Discussion points

What lessons in human nature can be learned from this scene?

What is the principle in your own life and how do attempt to practice it?

Comments;

**Life is eternal and love is immortal; And death is only a horizon,
And a horizon is nothing save the limit of our sight.**

Rossiter Worthington Raymond (1840–1918) was an American mining engineer, legal scholar and author. At his memorial, the President of Lehigh University described him as "one of the most remarkable cases of versatility that our country has ever seen—sailor, soldier, engineer, lawyer, orator, editor, novelist, story-teller, poet, biblical critic, theologian, teacher, chess-player—he was superior in each capacity. What he did, he always did well."

**Life is eternal. We should find this out, and begin
the demonstration thereof. . . Life is real and death is the illusion.**

Mary Baker Eddy (1821–1910), born to New England Puritan parents, was a devoted student of the Bible and sought for a healing system within it. Her discovery in 1866 of that system, which she named Christian Science, resulted in the amazing healings she performed and is recorded in the textbook *Science and Health with Key to the Scriptures* (1875). She founded the Church of Christ, Scientist in 1879, and the Christian Science Publishing Society (1898), which publishes periodicals including *The Christian Science Monitor* (in 1908).

Scene 3 tackles the question of life that continues

Death is no more than passing from one room into another.

Helen Adams Keller (1880 – 1968) was an American author, political activist, and lecturer. She was the first deaf-blind person to earn a bachelor of arts degree. A prolific author, Keller was well-traveled and outspoken in her convictions. A member of the Socialist Party of America and the Industrial Workers of the World, she campaigned for women's suffrage, labor rights, socialism, antimilitarism, and other similar causes. She was inducted into the Alabama Women's Hall of Fame in 1971 and was one of twelve inaugural inductees to the Alabama Writers Hall of Fame on June 8, 2015.

**Of course you don't die. Nobody dies.
Death does not exist. You only reach a new level of vision,
a new realm of consciousness, a new unknown world.**

Henry Valentine Miller (1891–1980) was an American writer who broke with existing forms by developing a sort of semi-autobiographical novel. *Tropic of Cancer* (1934), *Black Spring (*1936), *Tropic of Capricorn* (1939) and *The Rosy Crucifixion* trilogy (1949–59), were banned in the United States until 1961.

ACT 1

Scene 3

Outside 1's classroom. Characters: 531, 532, 10, 342,9,39, 911.

531 comes stomping along in front of the curtains with 532 after him.

> ### 531
> Imagine that. Telling me I can't count on statistics! That's the name of the game.

> ### 532
> But 411 said that just one number can make a tremendous difference.

> ### 531
> Do you have to repeat everything you hear? Maybe we need a new strategy, a new game plan.

He begins to leave stage.

> ### 532
> He said we don't need a new game plan, just use our abilities: reliability, believability, accountability, dependability, capability, stability, respectability.

She follows him off stage as she says this.
As they hurry across stage 10 passes them. She stops, turns and looks after them thoughtfully. She hears a siren and sees numbers running toward her, 342, 9 and 39.

> ### 39
> Did you hear, Number 10? Some number was erased. Maybe he erased himself.

> ### 10
> Oh, that's terrible. He should have called 988 for help. She and her team are so comforting. They might have changed his mind and saved him.

911 appears and takes emergency hat from the hat-tree marked, 911's hats.

> ### 911
> I'm 911 and I was called in to handle this emergency. I'm going to be taking statements. What happened? Was it a bus and who was driving?

No, no. It wasn't a bus. Number 181 was
erased by another number. Rubbed out
on purpose. I know all the details. He
had a lot of expensive jewelry. Why, he
even had the Hope diamond!

Others say, oooh, while 911 begins to write in his notebook.

911
Did anyone know the erased?

9
I interviewed him once and he didn't have
the Hope diamond. He had the diamond
of hope, and pearls of wisdom. He had
stocks in important companies too. Yeah,
he had lots of shares.

911
What kind of shares did he have?

9
He had shares in well...things like the
patience and kindness companies.

911
And just where did he keep his shares?

9
Oh, he didn't keep them. He shared his
shares with every number he met. No
matter who they were. Said he never
met a number he didn't like. So why did
someone erase him?

911
Evidently, some unscrupulous, crooked
number had the wrong idea about being
a number of substance. He thought it
was made up of chalk. Acting on that
erroneous supposition, he committed this
heinous crime and purposefully erased
Number 181, hoping to steal the jewels of
character 181 possessed.

Stops writing and shakes his head in confusion.

911
Mmm.. .my conclusion is, this was not
only a crime of envy, but one of idiocy too!
Now, I'd better read you your rights.

39

What do you mean, read us our rights?
We're just innocent bystanders.

911

Precisely, so you have the right to know
the truth about numbers.

911 sings rap song.

"RAP SONG"

Rubbed out, there is no doubt
Yeah, and I tell you no lie.
Rubbed out, without a doubt,
But who could have done it and why?
He gave all he had, he wasn't that bad
He really wasn't asking for this.
He gave all he had, but don't you be sad
Or what you should know you will miss.

(342 says, **What's that?**)

Life isn't a waste, it can't be erased,
It goes on and on no matter what.
Life isn't a waste, it can't be erased,
To know that will help you a lot.

342

What do you mean life goes on and on, no
matter what?

911

Well the Principle of Math is the life of
all numbers and does it have a beginning
or an end? Remember, numbers are
supposed to demonstrate what their
Principle is like.

10 speaks aside to Number 9 as others talk.

10

Of course, some numbers seem to do this
a little more perfectly than others.

9

Is that a mathematical fact, Number 10?

10

I'm not dealing with absolute facts
here perhaps, but at least perfection by
reputation. (Sighs). Oh, well, I'm still
unraveling that problem.

Others in the background are now heard talking.

342
I don't think I'm following him. We
should call a meeting on this, so we can
ask for directions. Are you a little lost
too, Number 39?

39
No, I don't believe I could be lost. It's not
the odd thing to do. We might meander a
little, but asking for directions really isn't
necessary. Odd numbers don't need a
whole lot of detail.

342
Well, I like detail. Could you detail that
for us, Number 911?

911
Sure, it's always good to clean up stuff
like misunderstandings. Let's see, does
anyone here have a mirror?

10
I do.

She gives mirror to 911

911
Hmm, what a surpise! Now, everyone,
see your reflection? It has to do what you
do, right?

He passes the mirror around and they all nod and agree.

911
So, if we use the Science of numbers like
a mirror and look into it, we'll find that
numbers are the reflections of Principle.
If our Principle is Truth, with a capital
T, then we have to reflect it. We have to
be truthful and honest. And if we reflect
Life, with a capital L then....

At this point 5 runs across the stage dribbling his ball in among the numbers.

342
And what are you doing here, Number 5?

5
Why do numbers keep asking me that?

342
We're having a serious discussion and you wouldn't fit into it.

5
Why not?

342
We're discussing life. And you're too . . . well, lively!

5
And they use me as an example of wrong addition, huh! I'm going to find some numbers who really want me. That's what I'm going to do. Goodbye!

5 bounces his ball off stage again.

39
Just a minute, let me get this straight. If Principle doesn't begin or end, how could a number begin or end? I mean even if chalk disappears.

342
Oh, I see what you're saying. 181's _true_ identity wasn't rubbed out.

911
Right! A number is really an idea and a good idea can't be erased.

9
Hey, that's great news. I could do a report on it.

911
And you can report that 181 is making progress because he still has to solve the problem of what life is, and who he really is in Numberland. He's just in a new school district, in continuing education.

10
So erasure isn't fatal. It only looks fatal to the numbers who see it, or hear about it. It's a Chalkland and not a Numberland view!

That's why you don't have the right to
remain silent. You've got a right to be
happy. Now, you're free to go... to go on
learning about life.

911 hands mirror back to 10 and they all walk off talking quietly but happily.
10 lags behind and looks at herself in the mirror again. 10 talks and sings "In
the mirror."

"IN THE MIRROR"

Spoken
**He said it's like looking in a mirror, that
numbers are the reflections of Principle.
But when I look in this mirror. . .**

Sung
**What's this reflection in the mirror I see
The one that is looking right back at me?
Does it hint at a truth that I never knew
Does it say there's more to me and to you?
It looks like me and it moves like me,
Why aren't I happy with what I see?**

Spoken
**But he said if we look into the Science of numbers,
We'll see what we're really like.**

Sung
**Could I look in a mirror that's different today
The Science that surely would show me the way,
To know what's really true about me
The number that we just can't quite see?**

Spoken
**And if I could see that, well, it would be
wonderful wouldn't it?**

Sung
**I'd reflect all that's good and loveliness pure,
The beauty of kindness, no Chalkland allure,
I'd be so happy with what I see
It's so like its Principle, this image that's me.**

Spoken with emphasis
Yes!

10 drops mirror off into a plant or a trash container as she exits stage, or she
may just go to side and be ready for the walk and sing group to approach her.

Discussion points

Do you feel that general ideas regarding death have changed over a number of years?

If "yes" then how?   Have you read any of the near death experiences people have survived to tell about?

Do you agree with the quotations that introduce this chapter? If "yes" or "no" give reasons or join the discussion

Comments:

**Along the way, let's never forget that once we were children
and that we were all playing together without distinction
of skin color, society level, or where people come from. We've
forgotten what that childlike experience was like.**

Guy Laliberté (born 1959), a Canadian businessman, investor, poker player and musician. In 1984, Laliberté founded Cirque du Soleil, a Canadian circus company whose shows have since been seen by more than 90 million people worldwide. In 2006, Laliberté was named the Ernst & Young Entrepreneur of the Year.

**Our evolution now requires us to develop spiritually - to become
emotionally aware and make responsible choices. It requires us to
align ourselves with the values of the soul - harmony,
cooperation, sharing, and reverence for life.**

Gary Zukav (born in 1942) is an American spiritual teacher and the author of four consecutive New York Times Best Sellers. Beginning in 1998, he appeared more than 30 times on The Oprah Winfrey Show to discuss transformation in human consciousness, concepts presented in his book *The Seat of the Soul*. His first book, *The Dancing Wu Li Masters* (1979), won a U.S. National Book Award.

Scene 4 deals with harmony in our relationships and with the color or race question

**None of us is responsible for the complexion of his skin.
This fact of nature offers no clue to the character
or quality of the person underneath.**

Marian Anderson (1897 – 1993) was an African-American contralto and one of the most celebrated singers of the twentieth century. She helped break the color barrier for black artists and was the first one to perform at the Metropolitan Opera in New York City in 1955. Her career was mostly spent in concert and recital venues throughout the U.S. and Europe between 1925 and 1965.

**I have a dream that my four little children will one day
live in a nation where they will not be judged by the color
of their skin but by the content of their character.**

Martin Luther King, Jr. as described before was a civil rights' activist of the 1960s. This quotation is from his famous, "I have a dream" speech, which has been quoted worldwide. King was assassinated in the tumultuous year of 1968, the same year as the president's brother, Robert Kennedy.

ACT 1

Scene 4

100 leads students walking on from stage left, all humming the intro to harmony song. 100 has the baton. All students are present except for 5. They stop stage center near 10.

100

Just remember that in Numberland your true self lasts forever and is totally in line with pure harmony. That's because the principle of music is the same as in math. Let's try it now with the words.

The class sings together.

"INTRO TO HARMONY"

**For harmony is true selfhood
It's absolutely pure.
It's held by perfect Principle
And ever will endure,
And ever will endure.**

531 Sings last line again but off key as everyone stares at him

531

And ever will endure!

9

Say, Number 531, have you thought of using your vocal talents in your campaign?

531

Well, no, I haven't. That's a great idea, Number 9. Write that down 532!

532 looks in the air and makes writing motions, but not doing it.

100

You're all improving. Keep going and you'll reach the key of happiness.

10

What's the key of happiness, Number 100?

33112

Well, I can't reach that key, because of my problem.

100

What's your problem, Number 33112?

33112

Oh, you wouldn't understand. No one
can.

Goes to side of stage and sulks.

342

How come when numbers have problems
they often say no one will understand? Is
it because they don't understand?

100

Perhaps it is. Oh Number 10, to reach
the key of happiness all we have to do
is be good to other numbers. You know,
be in harmony with others. And, uh, of
course we have to conform to the perfect
Principle of numbers.

10

Well, I used to think I was happy because
numbers tried to conform to me. But I
suppose that does have a minus side to it,
envy and stuff like that. And there are no
minuses in the key of happiness, right?
At least that's what someone told me.

531

Well, I don't need anyone to tell me what
makes 532 happy. She's loves to wave
those flags for me, don't you!

He makes a waving motion with both hands the way she used to but 532
shakes her head and holds the flags still against her. 531 looks unhappily
surprised. Then they hear cries from 5 of "help, help" and he comes in
staggering, all disheveled. 9 and 39 rush to help him as he collapses. Then
everyone clusters around him.

9

Are you alright Number 5? Speak to us!

532

Oh, someone do something. I think he's
fading. He may turn to chalkdust.

10

Number 5! Number 5! Can you hear me?
Stay with us, Number 5

100

Oh, Number 5. Think of your real nature,
the 5 that can't be erased. Think of that,
please.

Group

Yes, yes ....think of that Number 5.

The group continues to talk around 5 on the ground, motioning with their hands. 411 enters and comes to center stage. He addresses the audience.

411

Audience, we may need a little help
here. Would you please think of the true
Number 5, the one that isn't chalk. It's
the number that can never be in danger.
It can't be hurt or erased. Please think
only of that.

He leaves the stage while the group continues to talk silently to 5.

10

Remember, Number 5, the Principle of
math loves you and takes care of you.
The real you is alright. Try to understand
that. Please don't go.

5 begins to rouse and speaks weakly at first.

5

Where am I? Oh, hello everyone. What
happened? I felt like I was going on a
long journey and I saw a bright light and
Number 181 was there. He smiled at me.
I must have been dreaming. Then I heard
numbers calling me, so I woke up.

100

We're so glad you did Number 5. You're
needed here. And there's so much more
to learn about Numberland, and what we
really are.

532

It seems hard sometimes, doesn't it,
Number 5 but we're going to make it.
We'll graduate one day.

39

And besides, we want to see you play
ball some more. Maybe I'll teach you my
game.

5, sitting up and then standing with help.

5

Say, I'd like that. I want to learn a lot of new stuff.

100

Can you tell us what happened, Number 5? Where did you go and who did you meet?,

5

Well, it's kind of fuzzy. I wanted to join a group of numbers, but they didn't like the color of my chalk. Then they said I should try getting high. But I'm scared of heights, they make me dizzy. Next thing, they were all hitting me and well, I forget the rest.

100

Did those numbers all have minus signs on them?

5

Yes ...big, really big minus signs.

Makes a motion across his chest.

342

How can a number with a minus sign ever add up to anything? If you look at the details, obviously those minus numbers were dopey and dizzy.

532

They should have taken a government class like I did.

531

You took a government class? You didn't ask me, a politician, about government?

342

What did that teach you, Number 532? How would that help?

532

It helps because first of all you learn how to govern yourself. You use all your good resources. If you can't learn that basic skill then your life will be in chaos.

342

Chaos! Oh, just think of every day full of chaotic details. It's enough to make anyone dizzy.

39

That color class we took would have helped too, wouldn't it Number 9? We got asked some really hard questions like what's the color of intelligence or honesty? What's the color of kindness or friendship?

9

Right! Those minus numbers can't tell the color of anything except chalk. I'm going get hold of them and point out all their color mistakes, like this.

9 sings minus song and goes to various colors with his mike.

"COLOR SONG MINUS"

What's the color of your character,
The color of your thought?
Have you learned something wonderful,
Or just been badly taught?

For instance....Is your disposition boring brown,
Or envy's green hue?
Could you be a yellow who will run
Or might you just feel blue?
And....Is your anger colored real bright red
Or does it thunder black?
Do you turn a shade of purple
If others turn their back?

Or....
Do you think you could be white with fear
Or violet who will shrink?
If this is the case with numbers then
We should be colored pink.
Then we'd be in the pink.
Then we'd be tickled pink.

100

That's very clever, Number 9, except for one small thing.

9

What's that?

100
What right answers did you give? You
only pointed out their mistakes. That's a
start, but how will they learn from that?

10
So, how do we help other numbers?

100
Teach by example, by color of character.
See if you can pick up on this.

"COLOR SONG PLUS"

Number 100
What's the color of our character,
The color of our thought?

Number 39
We know it's something wonderful
For we've been so well taught.

Number 100
For instance,
The abundant green of nature's wealth
May very well be you.

Number 9
Or you could be sunny yellow joy
Or loyal as true blue.

Number 100
Or, **your nature may be lively red**
Or purple's noble hue,

Number 10
Friendly brown or loving shade of black
So good in all you do.

Number 100
Then again,
Your violet may be tender, kind
Indelible as ink.

Number 532
Or you could be white and pure as snow
Or happy tickled pink.
They all turn, point to 100 who is pink and all sing

She's happy tickled pink,
So we'll be tickling pink.   (They run off stage, while tickling Number 100)

Discussion points

Does this scene help with the race or color question? How?

How can these situations be better resolved?

Have you had difficult experiences or learned any hard life lessons along these lines? Have you found solutions?

Comments:

Your net worth to the world is usually determined by what remains after your bad habits are subtracted from your good ones.

Benjamin Franklin (1706 –1790), one of the Founding Fathers of the United States, was a leading author, printer, political theorist, politician, postmaster, scientist, inventor, civic activist, statesman, and diplomat. He was a major figure in the American Enlightenment, known for his discoveries and theories regarding electricity. Also known for the lightning rod, bifocals, and the Franklin stove. He facilitated Philadelphia's fire department and a university.

There is nothing noble in being superior to your fellow man; true nobility is being superior to your former self.

Ernest Miller Hemingway (1899 –1961) was an American novelist, short story writer, and journalist. His style, and life of adventure, had a strong influence on 20th-century fiction. Hemingway produced most of his work between the mid-1920s and the mid-1950s, and won the Nobel Prize in Literature in 1954. His works are considered classics of American literature: *The Sun also Rises; For Whom the Bell tolls; The Old Man and the Sea; A Farewell to Arms.*

Scene 5 handles the question of our own individual worth and challenges comparisons

Comparisons are odorous

Shakespeare produced most of his known work between 1589 and 1613. His early plays were primarily comedies and histories, and are regarded as some of the best work ever produced in these genres. He then wrote mainly tragedies until about 1608, including Hamlet, Othello, King Lear, and *Macbeth*. Lastly, he wrote tragicomedies, (romances), and collaborated with other playwrights. This quotation is from *Much ado about Nothing.*

We are shaped by our thoughts; we become what we think.
When the mind is pure, joy folllows like a shadow that never leaves.

Gautama Buddha, also known as Siddhārtha Gautama, Shakyamuni Buddha or the Buddha, was an ascetic and sage, on whose teachings Buddhism was founded. He is believed to have lived and taught mostly in the eastern part of ancient India between the sixth and fourth centuries BCE. He is recognized by Buddhists as an enlightened or divine teacher who attained full Buddhahood, and shared his insights to help sentient beings end rebirth and suffering.

ACT 1

Scene takes place in classroom. Number 1 and 911 enter and talk at stage left.

1

Hello 911. I hear you're substituting in the true worth class today.

911

Yes, I'm an emergency fill-in. But I have so many hats to wear, taking statements, keeping order and now, substitute teaching.

He takes a mortar board from his hat-tree marked 911,

1

You may have to keep order here. The trouble spot is due right about now. As for all those hats, haven't you heard the latest Chalkland expression? It's called multi-tasking.

911

What does that mean?

1

It means you do everything.

Pointing at 911 as he walks off

911

Oh. What trouble spot? Should I wear my hard hat? Hey, wait a minute!

He runs off stage after Number 1 as they exit stage left. All 8 students enter and replace chairs if necessary. They stand around talking. Number 5 pulls at a number and says.

5

Say, I've wondered about something.

Number 5 goes from one number to another singing. They all ignore him.

"WONDERING ABOUT WORTH"

**I've wondered what I'm really worth
Have you wondered too?
I feel that I'm diminished
When I'm compared with you.**

All numbers seem so very bright
Have you noticed too
I feel I just can't measure up
When I'm compared with you.

Do you have questions too?

He sings last line to audience, Buzzer sounds. They sit down. 911 enters, with percent sign, from stage left and raps on the desk to call the class to order.

911

Class, I'm 911 your substitute teacher for today. As a warm-up question, who can tell me an incorrect use of our resources? Yes, Number 532?

532

I've been thinking about color of character. Sincerity must be a clear, pure color, probably transparent because it has nothing to hide. So, it's insincere if you use a resource like kindness just because you want other numbers to like you. I think that's just doing a number on them.

Class titters and nudges each other.

531

Hold on, sincerity could be important. Perhaps 532 is right. I may have to follow her lead on that.

9

Follow her lead? How can he follow her lead? How can 531 follow 532? Wouldn't that upset things in Chalkland? We do have a system of values here, you know.

911

Let's do the lesson for today, it may help.

Glances at papers while class still is uneasy.

911

Oh, yes, I've got it. Now, in Numberland, in the real world of numbers, there's a law that says: Whatever benefits one number benefits all numbers.

He smiles around at class then frowns as heated conversations erupt.

342

This thing about all benefiting. How can that be?

39

Right! Aren't some numbers just more valuable than others? Haven't you seen my most valuable player trophy?

More noise and confusion ensue. 33112 raises her hand.

911

Class, class. Come to order please. Yes, uh, what is it, Number 33112?

33112

It's just a matter of prejudice, that's what I think it is. It's all those cute little numbers that get all the attention!

911

This may be a bit off the subject, but go ahead if you really feel the need.

33112

Do I feel the need! Do I feel the need! Where have you all been hiding yourselves? Don't you hear it, or are you just trying to tell me I'm imagining things, comments like, 'The ten best,' 'The top ten,' 'On a scale of one to ten,' and even 'The worst ten.' What is this love affair with single digits!

The class murmurs while 5 leans over and whispers loudly to 10.

5

Why, 10, on a scale of one to ten you would be last. And you're not even a single digit!

10

I'm just not going down that road anymore, Number 5.

911

Well, Number 33112, do you think your life would be so different if you were a single digit?

Of course, it would. I would get more respect. Why couldn't I have come onto the Chalkboard as an even single digit. For instance, I could have been 2, 4, 6 or 8. . .someone you appreciate. Oh, you just don't understand.

"33112'S LAMENT"

It's hard to be in my place
And know what I've been through,
You can't imagine my disgrace
'Cause I'm not simply 2.

It's true I'm blue
'Cause I'm not 2
My joys are all so few.

(Patter routine as per CD)

If I decide to buy some shoes
So pretty and so new
I feel embarrassed when they ask
Size 33112?

If I could be refigured then
My dreams might all come true
But I might end up fractionalized
Point 33112.

(Sings again)
It's true I'm blue
'Cause I'm not 2
Why can't I be like you?

(Patter routine as per CD)

All numbers when they're introduced
Say they'll remember you
One minute later they all say
3311 who?

I knock on single digits' doors
To tell what I've been through
I hear them say, don't open it,
It's 33112.

(Sings again)

It's true I'm blue
'Cause I'm not 2
There's nothing I can do.

I could have been a somebody
If I were more like you
I could have been a somebody
If I were simply 2.

She mutters loudly as she sits down.

33112

It's just prejudice. It's the P word.

911

You're taking things at face value. I know it's not easy to figure this out. It seems pretty natural to compare ourselves with other numbers. But you will find it puts our universe out of balance. So, now . . . I think you're all ready for the big question.

Class

The big question?

911

Where do comparisons take place? In Chalkland or in Numberland? Take a minute to discuss this.

Two groups form. 10, 33112, 531 and 532 are in one group to the side and the other four, 5,9,39 and 342 are in another group.

5

Is this a trick question?

9

Maybe it is, 'cause if we say comparisons take place in Numberland, wouldn't that be false reporting?

39

Sure, it's like saying the Principle of numbers plays favorites. Then it wouldn't be a perfect principle and where would that leave us? Maybe on the sidelines.

9

Not a good position. Well, what if we say comparisons only take place in Chalkland?

9 chuckles, satisfied.   342 answers slowly with sarcasm.

                          342
          Then 911 will say comparisons are
          temporary, like chalkdust. We'd have to
          give up on comparisons, wouldn't we!

They scratch their heads and say "this is tough", "hard question." They stand
around looking so puzzled.

                          911
          Class, please return to your seats. Yes,
          what is it Number 9?

                          9
          Don't think I'm being argumentative
          about this, but . . . just for the sake of
          argument, I'd like to make a point.

                          911
          Yes?

                          9
          I know we shouldn't compare color or
          shape of chalk, but a general comparison
          of talents might be okay. For instance,
          there could be a group with a high
          percentage of talent, labeled "quite
          extraordinary."

He pulls percent sign to his side. She has been sitting on a chair near 911.

                          342
          Yes, that's true. And there could be a
          group labeled "quite ordinary." Generally
          speaking, of course. We wouldn't want to
          get specific.

She pulls the percent sign to her.

                          9
          But we could get specific if we need to
          discuss something like... extraordinary
          me.

They do a tug of war with percent sign.

                          342
          Or ...extraordinary me and, uh, ordinary
          you.

Percent sign runs to 911.

9 and 342 sing and act out, "Extraordinary me and ordinary you."

"EXTRAORDINARY ME AND ORDINARY YOU"

Both
Extraordinary me
And ordinary you
What a pair we could make
What a scintillating two.

She with hands up in front of him

You would shine all the brighter
Because you're close to me.

He takes her hands and dances her backwards.

You would follow when we dance
What a pleasure that would be.

Both sing and she could sit on his knee

Extraordinary me
And ordinary you
Here's a dummy and mate
What a fascinating two.

He motioning as though he has strings on a puppet

I will pull strings for you
I'll speak the words you say.

She
But the glory will be mine
Thanks! You really made my day.

Both
Extraordinary me
And ordinary you
What a hit we would make
When I sing a song to you.

She
I would sing oh so sweetly
You'd hardly know it's me.

He
That would not be hard to tell
It would surely be off-key.

Both
Extraordinary me
And ordinary you
What a lot we will win
On the quiz show that we'll do.

He
There'll be so much applause
For the smarter of the two.

She
And the one they will applaud
You can bet it won't be you.
Both
Extraordinary me
And ordinary you
The distinction is quite clear
When comparisons you do.

Students repeat the last two lines in singing and acting. There is a longer dance version in the music accompaniment CD. 9 and 342 take their seats.

911
Let's think this through. How does our
Principle see numbers? Does it compare
them? Does it think of one number or one
group as more valuable than the other?
Could we drop out one number and still
have a balanced mathematical universe?

Class
No. No. I don't think so. Maybe not.

33112
Oh, I see! If we took out 688 where would
that leave 687 and 689? There'd be a
missing link in the chain of numbers.

Everyone agrees.

9
Chalkland would probably send out
search parties and go digging round for it.

They laugh but 33112 is still thoughtful.

33112
So every number is every bit as important
and valuable as another? Oh, that's
the truth in Numberland, isn't it! And
Chalkland will just have to wake up and
recognize the truth, won't it!

911

Yes, it will! So, let's go out and put
that into practice! And we can begin
by erasing comparisons. Remember,
in Numberland your numbers may be
different, but you're all of equal value or
worth.   Class dismissed.

911 exits and the students straggle out of classroom, two at a time, talking.

532

Without comparisons, we could
concentrate on the issues.

531

Good idea. We should figure the
percentage of valuable programs
available. So we'll need the percent sign.
Better put it back on the list.

532 smiles and writes on her pad. 531 pats head of percent sign. It smiles.

39

I suppose in the big game of life, no one
has to sit it out on the bench. So maybe
every player is valuable?

342

Uh-huh, including blue numbers.

39 and 342 walk out talking and smiling. 5 pulls at 9's sleeve.

5

I don't care if a single digit isn't special.
I just don't wanna be used anymore in
wrong arithmetic.   Why can't they use
some other number, like you Number 9?

9

It's too much work to go from 5 to 9.
Chalkland does it the other way round.
Now, let's not forget that geometry
meeting tomorrow. We could liven things
up a bit. I have a plan.

5

Do we have to go on a bus?

9

Of course not! What you are talking
about? Listen to me, c'mon. . .

Voices fade out as 5 and 9 walk off stage together and 33112 and 10 are left.

33112

I'm beginning to feel a little different
about myself, Number 10. I know you
had to figure this out too, but maybe from
the other side of the problem. What I
mean is uh, I heard you used to be um,
overly perfect.

10

But under perfect or over perfect are just
Chalkland comparisons, and they're both
wrong. I think true mathematics is a
matter of well . . .

"IT'S A MATTER OF. . ."

It's a matter of reflection
And it's very plain to see
That the good I see in others
Is the good that's here in me.

It's a matter of decision
For I know it to be true
That the good you do for others
Is the good that's here for you.

It's a matter of perfection
Which one day I hope to see
But that this is our true nature
Is the thought that comforts me.

And you will be comforted too
There's no one more loved than you.

It's a needed liberation
And the truth that sets us free
Is that Principle and numbers
Are as perfect as can be.

33112

As perfect as can be?

This line is spoken

10

10 sings   **As perfect as can be.**

10 puts her arm around 33112's shoulders and they walk off stage together.

INTERMISSION

Discussion points

Do you agree with the idea that comparisons of people are not helpful in life? Why do you agree or not agree?

What is the difference between healthy and unhealthy competition? What do they both produce?

In what ways do the characters in this scene change for the better? And does that help us?

You will never find a truly happy self-centered person.
They simply don't exist.

Hilary Hinton "Zig" Ziglar (1926 – 2012) was an American author, salesman, and motivational speaker. He was born in Coffee County in southeastern Alabama and was the tenth of 12 children. Navy College Training and the University of South Carolina. Ziglar later worked as a salesman. His books include, *See you at the Top* (1975) and *Born to Win: Find Your Success Code* (2012).

Nothing can stop the man with the right mental attitude
from achieving his goal; nothing on earth can
help the man with the wrong mental attitude.

Thomas Jefferson (1743 – 1826), an American Founding Father, was the principal author of the Declaration of Independence and later served as the third President of the United States from 1801 to 1809. He was elected the second Vice President, serving under John Adams, from 1797 to 1801. He was a proponent of democracy, republicanism, and individual rights motivating American colonists to break from Great Britain and form a new nation.

Act 11, Scene 1 depicts how to deal with negative thoughts and mental influences

The battle was no longer with people and circumstances
but with false thinking which was constantly being corrected
and defeated by true thinking.

John H. Wyndham (1906-1979), born in Holland. Served as a Liaison officer in Royal Australian Air Force in Second World War. Prisoner of war in the South Pacific for three years. His account of those years, his years in business and with the United Nations all make for gripping, inspiring reading in his book *The Ultimate Freedom*. For ten years, Wyndham lectured worldwide in packed venues such as Carnegie Hall, showing spiritual solutions to life's problems.

Once you replace negative thoughts with
positive ones, you'll start having positive results.

Willie Hugh Nelson (born April 29, 1933) is an American musician, singer, songwriter, author, poet, actor, and activist. He was one of the main figures of outlaw country, a subgenre of country music that developed in the late 1960s. Nelson has acted in over 30 films, co-authored several books. He wrote hit songs such as "Funny how Time Slips Away," "On the Road Again," and "Crazy."

ACT 11

Scene 1

411 enters. Later all 8 students enter, also 911 and teachers 1 and 100.

411

Here I am again, Number 411, to make
an important announcement. It's almost
time. Today, at exactly 5, the students
will meet so they can be introduced to
geometry and they will.....

5's ball rolls onto the stage. 411 stops it with his foot, or picks it up.

411

Number 5?   . . . 5, is that you?

5

You called me?

5 runs on stage.

411

No, I didn't call you.

5

Oh yes, you did, everyone heard it!

411

I was announcing the time. It had
nothing to do with you.

5

I never get called for anything important.
Maybe I'll start taking the percent sign
around.

411

Why would you do that?

5

100 got a lot of attention when she took it
around.

411

Number 5, you're supposed to be and do
good, not just look good. Anyway, I don't
think it would have quite the same effect.
I mean, 5 percent?

5

Well, I'm gonna think about it anyway.

411
Alright, fine, you go do that.

As 5 turns he catches sight of percent sign stage rear and runs after it.

411
Now where was I? Oh, yes, our little
group of players is about to begin another
inning in the game of life. Let's see if they
can figure out this new angle and make it
to home base.

411 exits and 9 enters pulling 5 by the collar after him.

9
About our plan. Do you have the music?

5
Yes, but I don't have a singer yet.

9
Then find one.

All 8 students are on stage now and 9 takes center stage.

9
Students, your attention please. You
wanna know about geometry? I have an
angle on the subject. Here it is:
Oh, geometry, geometry
You really don't play fair
In circles you spin us round and round

He pauses   We like a dance that's square.
C'mon, c'mon everyone.

5
Quick.. emergency singer.

911 has walked in during the poem, 5 takes a cowboy hat off 911's rack, thrusts it and the music at 911 who takes it, puts on hat, looks puzzled but calls the square dance while students dance. There is a long and short version of the dance, longer has an extra verse without lyrics. 10 and 39 look around for partners and end up dancing together.

"SQUARE DANCE"

Pick your partner walk the line
Make an angle that's just fine
Circle left around the floor
Then the evens just all four.

Take your partner, one not two
A triangle just won't do
Square is in and cube is out
Why do students scream and shout?

Spin your partner one last time
You can have her, she's not mine
No one here is really free,
Captured by geometry.

As dance ends Number 10 and 39 stare at each other meaningfully. Then 1 and 100 enter and see 911.

> 100
> You conduct warm-up exercises, 911?   We
> could use him in other classes too.

Turns to 1 who nods. 911 takes hat off, hands it to 5, who hangs it up again.

> 911
> You're so helpful, Number 5.

> 1
> Students, we're here to give you a basic
> idea of geometry, which is all about the
> kind of thinking we do. What's our angle
> on life? Is it a right or wrong angle? Are
> we trying to bend angles to suit ourselves?
> But for starters, you need to realize
> that you are not the center of a circle.
> Everything does not revolve around you.

> 5
> It doesn't?

> 100
> No, it doesn't, Number 5. That's a
> common error on the Chalkboard. You
> can never reach the highest lesson or your
> better self if you believe that.

> 342
> What's the highest lesson?

> 100
> It's to figure out that our Principle is
> Love and so we have to be loving and
> kind. Believing you are the center of
> everything, or wanting to be popular, will
> stop you from learning that lesson. And
> you'll be just self-centered.

CLASS

Ooooh!

100

Number 1 can tell you about a number who had to learn this. I think it was that excellent and popular artist, Number 2021. Do tell them, Number 1.

1

Alright, I will.

"GETTING THE RIGHT ANGLE"

There once was a number with talents,
All his friends said, "Quite a few."
He really should paint a big picture,
Circle the Board with what he could do.
So he centered the spotlight on himself,
And chose his paint with care.
"I certainly know what I'm doing," he smiled,
"I surely have much to share."

But the circles became quite narrow,
His paint got mighty thin,
But still enough to make the rounds
And totally hem him in.

So,
He began again with center fixed
On Principle, which is Love,
He sought no other guidance
Than that which is above.

The circles began to widen
The paint became more bright
He knew the overflowing joy
Of simply doing right.

And he didn't even notice
So engrossed in work was he
That everyone whose life he touched
Shone with a marvelous radiancy.
A marvelous radiancy.

They all applaud.

100

Now, thinking he was the center of his world, gave that number a wrong not a right angle on life. Can anyone explain the difference?

Well, a wrong angle would be something
bad like selfishness. And a right
angle would be something good like
unselfishness.

1
Exactly! Remember, a right angle helps
you find answers to your important
questions.

5
Like who was driving the bus?

100
Why do you ask that, Number 5?

5
I donno. I think it was important, but I
forget why.

100
Keep listening, Number 5. If you really
need to know something, the answer will
come.

1
Yes, answers do come. That's called
inspiration. But here's the tricky part.
The answer doesn't begin with you.
Where can you find it?

531
I know now it's not in statistics. It has
to be somewhere in the Principle of
Mathematics. But that would mean
the answer is there before you ask the
question.

1
Excellent reasoning, Number 531. Now,
you've all had questions about odd and
even numbers. If you sign up for the
next geometry class you might find some
answers.

100
But for now some of you have an
assignment. Numbers 39, 10, 342 and
9 think about a presentation for the
defeating minuses class. And don't forget
to take out the minus trash.

Teachers and four students exit. 342 whispers to 10.

342

Do you get the feeling Number 39 really
likes you?

10

Yes, kind of. I think so. You know, he
does look different to me these days.
Can't think about that right now. Let's
see about these minus signs.

342

Look harmless, don't they?

9 flourishes one in her face and she backs away.

9

Careful, it might getcha.

They laugh as 911 enters.

911

Don't be afraid of minus signs. Just
throw them in the trash if you find any
lying around or if they are shot at you.

39

They can be shot at us?

911

Yes, sometimes minus signs are shot at
you on purpose, so you need to defend
yourself against them.

9

How do we do that?

911

By uncovering their disguise.

39

What kind of disguise do they wear?

911

Minus signs can be disguised as other
numbers, but their most deceptive
disguise that gives you the most trouble,
is when they come disguised as you.

He pokes 39 in the chest with a minus sign.

39

What do you mean?

911

Anytime you find yourself thinking or
saying, "I feel miserable, angry, sick,
resentful or unsuccessful"—you know
stuff like that, you can be sure a minus
sign is trying to attach itself to you. If it
succeeds you'll have that minus sign right
on the front of you. You'll be minus 39.
Listen!

911 sings

"MINUS WARNING"

Blmn. Blmn. Blmn.

Be careful what you think
Take care in what you do
Or else some little minus
Will attach itself to you.

It's not so hard to spot
That negativity
Choose good, uplifting thoughts
And then you will be free.

If anger, fear or doubt
Comes knocking at your door
Just slam it shut and shout
"You're not welcome anymore!"

Be wary of a minus
It'll stick to you like glue
And the worst part of that is,
It'll come disguised as you.

Come disguised as you.
Come disguised as you.

Blmn. Blmn. Blmn.

9

That sounds hypnotic.

911

That's how minus signs operate. They
hypnotize you.

39

I don't get it. What's behind a minus
sign? What's it all about?

911
Ah, you want to know the secret?

Group
Yes, yes. Tell us the secret.

911
Well, there's nothing, absolutely nothing
behind minus signs. Just a big zero.
Minus signs don't have any life of their
own, so that's why they try to take yours.
Don't give it to them and remember,
always take out the trash! Now, you'd
better work on your presentation.

911 exits and the four sift through the minus signs.

39
Why don't we just go into class with
a basket full of minus signs and show
them we're taking out the trash?

10
But what about the ones that have stuck
to us? They're really sticky.

They all think and say, hmm.

342
Oh, I just had an inspiration!

9
Without a long business meeting?

342
When you feel inspired you don't need
long meetings.

9
Really, tell me about it!

342
Okay, I will. Every time you hear a
minus statement, out loud or in your
head, just put a plus in its place.

9
Aha. Put a plus in its place. Hey wait
a minute! I just figured out how to
improve my news reporting. Cancel out
the minus news with plus news.

342

But what about our presentation?

9

I've got it! Let's take turns and make
up something minus to say, like about
school. Then the rest of us replace it
with a plus statement. Okay?

Group

Okay!

9

Good, then I'll start off.

Optional:
Zero (child) with basket of minus signs, tries to attach them and they are
pulled off. Zero gives up and throws signs in air and walks off.

DEFEATING MINUSES"
9 sings and holds minus sign in front of him or zero tries to attach it to him

Can I prove it—this perfection?
Can I figure what I truly am?
Is it certain, is it loving?
Could there really be a perfect plan?

The others reply by singing and at end 342 pulls minus sign away

Our perfection is from Principle
And it's already true,
We can prove it step by little step
It's here for me and you.

342 sings and holds minus sign in front of her or zero tries to attach it to her

There's so much to learn and my teacher's stern
I fear I just may fail,
I'm lost at sea, can you rescue me
Cause I don't know how to bail.

The others sing and at end 39 pulls the sign away from 342

You must steer towards the shore of love
And then you cannot fail,
Catch the winds of hope, the tides of joy
And they will help you sail.

39 sings and hold sign in front of him or zero tries to attach it to him

I speculate, can I graduate.
Can I deal with all this chalk?

I've sealed my fate, can't assimilate
It just seems like so much talk.

Others reply and at end 10 takes the minus sign from 39

There's no progress when you speculate
From basis of this chalk,
You must face what's true, the real you,
Be done with all chalktalk.

10 holds up sign for only a moment, throws it in air, or zero gives up, throws signs in air and exits.

I can add up? I can figure?
I can find out what I truly am.
So, it's certain and it's loving,
And there really is a perfect plan.

All four of them sing

Yes, the truth that we can understand,
Which chalk just cannot hide,
Is that good is here for all of us
And ever will abide.
And ever will abide.

39 and 9 have a mock sword fight with minus signs which 10 and 342 finally put in trash. Exit.. 5 enters alone and speaks confidentially to audience.

5

I was just thinking. It's not too much
work to go from 5 to 9 is it?   So if
you want to use an example of wrong
arithmetic you could say, "That's just like
saying 4 and 4 are . . .9. See, isn't that
easy?

411 enters.

411

What are you doing out here, 5?

5

Oh, nothing. I was just sharing
something helpful.

411

Really? Well, anything worthwhile is
based on the Principle of numbers, or else
it's just a chalk opinion. So, is this from
Principle?

5 mumbles as he looks down at his feet

5

Well, maybe not exactly from Principle.

411

What's that, I don't hear you?

5 looks up in the air.

5

Maybe not exactly from Principle.

411

So you were just engaging in chalktalk, was that it? Spreading a little more chalkdust around?

411 puts his arm on 5's shoulder.

411

Now 5, it doesn't matter what Chalkland says about you. You're an important part of mathematics. The audience knows that.

5

They do?

411

Of course. Just listen. Audience, what is 2 plus 3?

He holds out his hands for an answer. Audience says "5".

411

There! See how are necessary you are.

5

Well, that does help. But I'm still thinking about the percent sign.

411

Maybe you'd better be thinking about the next scene. I believe you're in it.

5

Oh, (gasps) you're right!

5 rushes off stage.

411

Interesting isn't it. In Chalkland,
numbers could actually miss their cue to
take part in something worthwhile, while
worrying about things that really don't
matter at all.

411 exits stage

Discussion points

What effect does self-centered thinking have on the person and their work or family circles?

How important a place does thinking hold in our lives? Why?

Do negative people make friends easily or do others avoid them? Why?

You may have heard the idea of "change your thinking, change your life." Do you believe this to be true? Why?

Is it possible to make a habit of challenging our own negative thoughts and replacing them with better ones? What are the results?

When men and women agree, it is only in their conclusions; their reasons are always different.

Jorge Agustín Nicolás Ruiz de Santayana y Borrás, known in English as George Santayana (1863 – 1952), was a philosopher, essayist, poet, and novelist. Originally from Spain, Santayana was raised and educated in the United States from the age of eight and identified himself as an American. Santayana influenced those around him, including Bertrand Russell, T. S. Eliot, Robert Frost, Gertrude Stein, and Supreme Court Justice Felix Frankfurter.

Sometimes I wonder if men and women really suit each other. Perhaps they should live next door and just visit now and then.

Katharine Houghton Hepburn (1907 – 2003) was an American actress. Known for her fierce independence and spirited personality, Hepburn was a leading lady in Hollywood for more than 60 years. She appeared in a range of genres, from screwball comedy to literary drama, and she received four Academy Awards for Best Actress—a record for any performer. In 1999, named by the American Film Institute as the greatest female star of Classic Hollywood Cinema.

Scene 2 tackles the age-old question of male and female compatibility

When men and women are able to respect and accept their differences then love has a chance to blossom.

John Gray (born 1951) is an American relationship counselor, lecturer and author. In 1969, he began a nine-year association with Maharishi Mahesh Yogi before beginning his career as an author and personal relationship counselor. In 1992 he published the book *Men Are from Mars, Women Are from Venus,* which became a long term best seller and formed the central theme of all his subsequent books. His books have been bought in the millions around the world.

We hold these truths to be self-evident, that all men and women are created equal.

Elizabeth Cady Stanton (November 12, 1815 – October 26, 1902) was an American suffragist, social activist, abolitionist, and leading figure of the early women's rights movement. Her Declaration of Sentiments, presented at the Seneca Falls Convention held in 1848 in Seneca Falls, New York, is often credited with initiating the first organized women's rights and women's suffrage movements in the United States. Stanton was president of the National Woman Suffrage Association from 1892 until 1900.

Scene 2

Geometry classroom and all students will be present with Number 1 and 100.

Students walk into the geometry classroom as 10's love song melody is being played. Number 100 takes roll in background as 10 walks in singing her daydream love song. She pauses in the middle while accompaniment continues and at that point 39's number is called and he stands up. That is the only audible roll call. Audience sees other numbers standing up but it's all muted. As 10 finishes 100 calls her number and as music stops 100 calls her the second time loudly and everyone is staring at her. She's startled out of her daydream. The timing on this is very important.

"10'S LOVE SONG"

Why is my heart all aflutter?
Could there be something amiss?

100 calls out "39" and he answers "here"

And when his number they utter,
Why am I feeling like this?
Why do I dream of his kiss?
What is the angle on this?

100
(When music is almost at the end) 10? (Music stops). . .10?
(Listen to CD with dialogue for some of this timing.)

Everyone is staring at her. 10, looking very flustered, takes her seat).

10
Here.

100
Today we're going to tackle a big mystery.
Some of the best thinkers in Chalkland
have tried hard to solve the problem of
odd and even numbers, and they couldn't
do it.

9
How come?

1
Because they never got out of Chalkland
in all their calculations. Now, we'll start
off with a couple of questions. Number
39, what do you think of even numbers?

39

(Chuckles) Well, they're so well-rounded. Their shapes are very interesting to me, but their thinking puzzles me. They can just go off on tangents. Odd numbers don't do that.

(39 Sings Odd song.)

"ODD STATEMENT"

The odds are not like evens
I'm glad that it's quite true
The odds are not like evens
We're stable through and through.

Yes, evens change the subject
Just like they change their mind
They ask us endless questions
Then say that we're not kind.

I run a darn good foot race
I win in wrestling too
And even without trying
There's nothing an odd can't
Nothing an odd can't
Nothing an odd can't do.

He high five's Number 9 as he sits down.

100

And Number 33112, what do you think of odd numbers?

33112

They're kind of rugged, and sometimes that's reassuring to an even number and other times... it's well...just a little bit offensive. Oh, this subject always gives me trouble, so I really don't have any answers, just questions.

33112 Sings Even song

"EVEN ANSWER"

Why can't odds take direction?
Why won't they sit up straight?
Why do they give a challenge?
Why do they take the bait?

**I'll change to please another
My shape my make-up too
I'll be a whole new number
There's nothing I won't do.**

**Yes, odds are not like evens
I think it's all too true
The odds will not be evens
No, never like me and
Never like me and
Never like me and you.**
She motions to an even number. 1 and 100 smile at each other.

1
That's all chalktalk, that's all it is!

10
So, what's it like in Numberland? Are
odds and evens still different?

100
Yes and no. They do have some things in
common. What do you think they are?

9
Well, odds and evens are both complete,
whole numbers.

532
And odds and evens would have the same
resources so they'd all be... you know,
wise and strong and kind and gentle.

1
So far so good. But what makes odds and
evens different? Let me give you a clue.
It has to do with geometry angles and
how numbers think. There's a word for
thinking called "mentality."

39
Okay, using geometry, well, let's see...
maybe odds and evens have different
angles. Different ways of thinking. What
was it, oh yes, different mentalities. We
can't make them the same even if we try.

1
You're getting there, Number 39.
Different angles can be obvious in
Chalkland too, so what is their difference
in Numberland?

342

In geometry there are complementary
angles, aren't there? I have a feeling the
answer has to do with that.

10

Oh, yes, your'e right, Number 342.   In
Chalkland, odds and evens don't always
get along with each other because their
angles are different.   In Numberland,
their angles are still different but
complementary, so they'd always
harmonize, get along perfectly with each
other. Is that right?

1

That's correct, Number 10. You've
all come a long way. The Principle of
Mathematics is like, well, it's like a father
and a mother to numbers. So both odds
and evens are needed because they show
that. Number 100?

"ODD AND EVEN/CONGA LINE"

(100 begins by almost talking. Listen to CD for this song.)

Odd and even numbers I'm sure you'll all agree
Are good and true and perfect and whole as can be.
With even dispositions, they are tender, kind,
Oddly original because reflecting Mind.

(Number 1 continues)

Gone are all those factions and partiality
What is that you're saying about mentality?
Yes! That is the difference that odd and even show
That is so important for you all to know.

(Number 100 again)

Odd and even angles, it's just not so involved
The answer is quite simple, the mystery now is solved.
Odd and even angles complement each other
Principle needs those angles as our Father-Mother.

Then with music, pupils do a conga dance, with 5 at the end. When they turn
he gets left behind, and when he runs after them they turn back and are then
facing him and he has to walk backwards. Their hands on shoulder of person
in front of them. Then 5 turns around again, sees & follows percent sign
around stage, but ends up in the front of the line as the dance finishes.   There
are many ways of performing the dance. Class takes their seats.

1

You did very well with that. And remember, <u>in the real</u> world, <u>in</u> Numberland, all numbers have absolute equality... a totally level playing field.

100

That reminds me of an important graduation requirement. We have to be able to draw the line between what's real and what's not, between Numberland and Chalkland. So, as we finish this class please remember,

"NUMBERLAND"

100 sings first verse Numberland song.

Numberland is for certain where things always fit.
Chalkland is a maybe with so many "ifs."
So we had to ask you one question at a time
If you understand now just how to draw the line.

(Students sing)
Numberland is for certain where things always fit.
Chalkland is a maybe with so many "ifs."
But because you asked us one question at a time,
Yes, we understand now just how to draw the line.

Teachers wave and exit and students hum and break into two groups with 9 and 39 to the side. During the hummed verse of Numberland song this dialogue takes place. Please refer to CD for timing.

9

Say, Number 39, we're all meeting later.
Ask 10 to come too, won't you?

39 replies with feeling. It's a romantic line.

39

Sure, fine. Yes, I'll uh, ask 10.

Then he sings

So, I need to ask you one question at a time
If, perhaps that maybe you ever could be mine.

 At this point the students all chat. 39 stands off to the side and sings "39's Love Song" and during the third verse 10 turns in his direction and waves and he waves back.)

If I told you that I love you
Would you know it to be true?
Would you still want me around you,
Or would you just say we're through?

If I told you you're more perfect
Than you ever were before.
Would you listen and believe me
And would you then want me more?

If you looked in my direction
I would have to ask you this.
Do you think it would be alright
Just to give me one small kiss?

If I told you that I love you. . .

10 leaves group and goes forward as 39 holds out his hand to her. She takes it. They walk to the side of the stage and talk quietly.

33112

Number 1 said we all have a level playing field. It's a matter of equal opportunity. That means I have the same chance everyone else has to do something good for other numbers. So, is there a place for me to volunteer in your company, Number 342?

342

There certainly is, Number 33112. In fact, we need someone to head up a new department. It's called volunteering for the good of the neighborhood. Would you be interested in that?

33112

Oh, I certainly would. Thank you. The game of life is better than I thought. Maybe it's because of the level playing field.

9

The best games are always played on a level playing field.

The others agree as 911 comes out towards hat-tree, picks it up as though to removes it, hears what is said and puts it down again. Talks mostly to himself.

911

A level playing field? Huh, that could
mean an equal distribution of hats.

911 takes hats off hat-tree and hands them to other numbers as they walk off.
Begins with 33112, 342, then 9 as they walk off. 532 and 531 talk.

531

That's the kind of platform we could stand
on. An honest-to-goodness level playing
field.

532

Honest-to-goodness. Oh, I like the sound
of that. Shall I write it down?

531

No, I'll remember it. Honesty and
goodness.

He takes the two flags from 532 as he says each word, honesty, goodness.

531

Think I'm going to have to wave those
flags myself.   After you.

531 motions for her to leave and 532 looks pleased. 911 hands 532 and 531
hats as they walk off. 5 is trailing after them.

5

A really level playing field? Wow! I've
never seen one of those in Chalkland.
Where is it? I could play ball there.

911 puts one hat on his head and hands last hat to 5, dusts his hands off, and
he exits taking empty hat tree. 39 and 10 are on side of stage, where they talk.

39

Number 10, I have a confession to make.

10

What's that Number 39?

39

This may come as a surprise to you, but
umm, I don't think I've always allowed for
the even angle.

10

Oh?

39

Somehow I thought all the even numbers
would become, well . . . odd like me.
S'pose that does surprise you.

10

Not really. I've had odd thoughts about
the odds too, that they should be more...
oh, you know, even-handed in what they
do. I just never understood their angle.

39

Geometry isn't easy, is it! And something
else. I lived for competition. I don't want
to use this as an excuse, but odd numbers
are used to competing with each other.
After all, it _is_ the odd thing to do.

10

Oh, it certainly is. But even numbers
have problems too. Before I came to this
school, l believed everything Chalkland
told me about beauty and how to be
evenly perfect. But that was all illusion
and not reality at all. Guess I just wanted
to be loved.

39

I've been wondering about love, Number
10. What do you think it is?

10

Mmm. What I used to call love was
probably chalk hopes and fears all mixed
together. But now... the best kind of
love we can have for each other? I think
it's when we understand and value each
number's real nature.

39

How do you figure we do that?

10

I'm not totally sure. But I did find out
that things like goodness, intelligence or
real beauty don't belong to any particular
number. They're available for all of us.
You know, like the percent sign.

39

Oh, I see. It's like that mirror example.
It's a matter of reflection, isn't it!

10
Yes, yes it is!

39 and 10 sing the reprise,

IT'S A MATTER OF REFLECTION...

It's a matter of reflection
And it's very plain to see
That the good I see in others
Is the good I see in me.

It's a matter of decision
For I know it to be true
That the good you do for others
Is the good that's here for you.

It's a matter of perfection
Which one day I hope to see
But that this is our true nature
Is the thought that comforts me.

And you will be comforted too
There's no one more loved than you.

It's a needed liberation
And the truth that sets us free
Is that Principle and numbers
Are as perfect as can be.

5 comes rushing by.

39
Hold on Number 5. Why are you rushing
around?

5
We're supposed to meet for a farewell
song, but I can't go till I find....

10
Till you find what, 5?

5
I can't tell you.

He rushes off stage

39
One of life's little mysteries. He must
think it's very important.

Or maybe it's about being important.
But he already is, he just doesn't know it
yet. Let's go so we're not late. Number 1
always says it's kind to be on time.

They exit stage.

Discussion points

Does the geometry explanation help us to understand the different angles or mentalities that men and women have?

Can these be different but still equal?

What does equality mean?   Equal pay for same job?   Are men and women required to do the same jobs in the same way as each other.   Is that possible?

Do the conclusions or remarks of Number 10 and Number 39 help us in our own search for a better understanding of each other? How?

**A flower cannot blossom without sunshine, and man
cannot live without love.**

Friedrich Max Müller (1823 –1900), generally known as Max Müller, was a German-born philologist and Orientalist, who lived and studied in Britain for most of his life. He was one of the founders of the western academic field of Indian studies and the discipline of comparative religion. Müller wrote both scholarly and popular works on the subject of Indology.

**You will find as you look back upon your life
that the moments when you have truly lived are
the moments when you have done things in the spirit of love.**

Rev. Prof Henry Drummond (1851 –1897) was a Scottish evangelist, biologist, writer and lecturer. Few men exercised more religious influence in their own time, especially on young men. He became famous for his *Natural Law in the Spiritual World,* (1883) but perhaps his most lasting legacy is, *The Greatest Thing in the World,* a comparison of faith, hope and love in 1 Corinthians 13.

*The final scene reveals the love that never changes
and how we grow into that love*

Love is the crowning grace of humanity, the holiest right of the soul,
the golden link which binds us to duty and truth, the redeeming
principle that chiefly reconciles the heart to life,
and is prophetic of eternal good.

Francesco Petrarca (1304 – 1374), anglicized as Petrarch, was an Italian scholar and poet in Renaissance Italy, whose rediscovery of Cicero's letters is often credited with initiating the 14th-century Renaissance. Petrarch is often considered the founder of Humanism, which emphasizes the value and agency of human beings, and affirms their ability to improve their lives through reason and ingenuity as opposed to submitting blindly to tradition and authority.

**And now these three remain: faith, hope and love.
But the greatest of these is love.**
1 Corinthians 13, NIV

"If I speak in the tongues of men or of angels, but do not have love, I am only a resounding gong or a clanging cymbal....Love is patient, love is kind. It does not envy, it does not boast, it is not proud...Love never fails. But where there are prophecies, they will cease; where there are tongues, they will be stilled; where there is knowledge, it will pass away."

Scene 3

Scene takes place in classroom. All are present except for 5.

100

Hello everyone. You've made real
progress but graduation doesn't happen
overnight. It's more like gradually
waking up to what's real. Numberland
appears and Chalkland is left behind in
the dust. But before this can happen the
greatest lesson of all must be learned and
put into practice. Number 1?

She turns and 5 comes rushing past with the percent sign in tow. He beams
triumphantly. Number 1 smiles and holds up his hands in a pleasant inquiry
fashion.

1

The most important lesson in life is
love—love that isn't chalk, that doesn't
crumble in the sun or melt in the rain.
This kind of love might come through us
but it doesn't come from us It comes from
our Principle, which is always telling
us, "It's forever that I love you." This is
something we should never forget.

1 sings, "It's forever that I love you."

ITS FOREVER THAT I LOVE YOU

It's forever that I love you.
Do you know this to be true,
Do you listen to the angels
That I am sending you.

For in my eyes you are perfect
And you evermore will be.
But appearances are fleeting
They are not the truth I see.

There is no purer love
Than what I have for you.
If you don't know me now
You will when joys are few.

So if it takes ten moments
Or even ten long years,
I'll be right here to hold you
And wipe away your tears.

Love is only an illusion
When it seems to come and go
But the love that never changes
Is the greatest truth you'll know.

There is no life without loving
And the fear this could exist
Will just vanish into nothing
As the sun dispels the mist.

During bridge he could pat 5's head the percent sign, and shake hands etc.

Though you may have never known me
I have been here all along,
And one day you will agree that
It's with me you do belong.

It's forever that I love you.

Students applaud.

1
Goodbye everyone, goodbye.

He exits followed by 100.

GROUP
Goodbye Number 1, goodbye.

The students follow slowly, waving to their teacher giving him time to make
a quick change and return as Mr. Goodman. The background dims and the
spotlight falls on 411, stage right, as the group exits stage left. He looks at
them as they leave. 5 breaks away and comes running back to 411.

5
Is this the end of the play?

411
Just about.

5
And I didn't do anything special.

411
Oh, yes you did. You were the only one
who remembered all the way through
that it was a play. You see, Number
5, Chalkland is a stage and our parts
improve as we improve. Think about that,
okay?

5

Okay. But how do we get back out of the play? I don't even know how we got here.

411

We never go back, Number 5, only forward. And the way to do that is to learn our lessons. For instance, I had a big one to learn.

5

What do you mean, Number 411?

411

Well, I had so many facts in my head that I was given the part of the Narrator, and not one of the characters. It sidelined me. I've had to learn that just knowing facts doesn't mean much. It's the right facts put into practice that count. Did you learn something about yourself too, Number 5?

5

Well, yes, I guess so. I kind of had to admit to myself that catching the percent sign really didn't make me important. Actually, I felt a bit silly. I think I'll ask Number 100 to tutor me in math.

411

That's a very good and humble idea. I think you're ready to exit the play now.

5

I am? Oh....

Pauses & looks at 411 sadly.

5

Well, then uh, goodbye Number 411.

411

Goodbye, Number 5.

5

Goodbye, everyone.

5 speaks that line to audience. 411 watches 5 exit then turns to audience.

411

Our numbers may not have completely
solved the problem of being but they have
made some progress, haven't they? Chalk
walls of ignorance, prejudice or hate don't
fall immediately, but real love finally
dissolves them. That's the truth, and the
truth always wins. After all, the school
motto is T.T.—Truth Triumphant.

411 makes T.T. with his two index fingers and walks to side of stage, ready to
exit but turns and adds.

411

So, dear audience, we wish you Godspeed
in this journey we're taking together. No
one truly travels alone and yes, we really
are loved. Remember us, remember
Numberland, remember, remember.....

His voice trails off, lights dim on him or he exits, and we see the teacher in
actual classroom, his back to audience, waving goodbye to his pupils, but they
are not visible.

MR. GOODMAN

Remember, remember you can do it. You
can put it all into practice. You'll be okay.
You'll succeed.

He turns to face audience and begins packing up his books. Background music
of "Let go of your burden," plays and whole sequence is timed to coincide with
the music. Teacher looks at percent sign and other classroom effects. In a
minute Andy enters with a knock at the door. Little Helper is with him.

ANDY ABLE

Just wanted to double check with you
Glen if the lights have been up to the max
in brightness these last few classes.

MR. GOODMAN

Oh, yes thank you Andy. The lights are
fully on.

ANDY

You're packing it all up now, huh?

MR. GOODMAN

Last day of this class.

ANDY

We'll help take down some of the stuff.

Helper and he go to work.

ANDY
So...was it a good class?

MR. GOODMAN
Oh, it was a great class the way it all
finally turned out. But they left with
hardly a word to me... except goodbye.

ANDY
Maybe they just don't know how to say
they're grateful.

MR. GOODMAN
Speaking of gratitude, thanks a lot for all
the help you've given. Haven't seen you
rushing around so much lately.

Helper takes down percent sign from wall and looks at it lovingly.

ANDY
Yup, I realized that when you do work
that belongs to someone else you both lose
a percentage of success. At least that's
what I heard. A wise woman said it.

MR. GOODMAN
Sounds like good advice. Speaking of
percentage, how are you doing today,
Gus? Still like to do math?

GUS
Oh, yes, Mr. Goodman, and I learned a lot
by seeing your class in action.

MR. GOODMAN
Really, what was that?

LITTLE HELPER
Well, about fifty percent of the world's
population is girls and women. So, they
should have an even playing field, like
a good education. They'll have an equal
voice in the world one day, won't they?

MR. GOODMAN
Yes, they will, when the world learns to
love more and fear less.

LITTLE HELPER
And there's something else I need to tell
you.

MR. GOODMAN
What's that?

LITTLE HELPER
My name isn't Little Helper or Gus. My
name is really Augusta.

MR. GOODMAN
Pleased to make your acquaintance,
Augusta!

He bows and she curtsies. Knock at the door.

MR. GOODMAN
Come in.

T.D. enters

MR. GOODMAN
Oh, T.D. is there something else you
need?

T.D.
Yes sir, there is! The others are coming
in a minute, but I wanted to tell you that
after our math class I feel ready to tackle
well...almost anything. And not just on
the football field.

MR. GOODMAN
That's great T.D. I hope you'll write me
now and then and tell me how you're
doing. Oh, and you'd better address it
"Dear Teach" so I'll know it's from you.

T.D.
I sure will! Oh, here they come.

Looks around and the students in party clothes crowd around teacher,
hugging him.

PREZ
Mr. Goodman, I want to tell you about the
Community Campaign I'm organizing.
But it's not political. It was actually
Bonnie's idea to do helpful things for
our community, like repair and paint
as neeeded. We realized unselfish
projects are a way to have life add up
to mean something. Kitty will be our
spokesperson 'cause she's real unselfish.

BONNIE

And I'll do simple bookkeeping for it. Too many details slow things down. Serena's going to tutor neighborhood children in math.

FREDDIE

You're going to tutor me too, aren't you Serena?

SERENA

I certainly am. I'm just tickled pink to be tutoring! I love to help.

T.D.

We'll all help. Angela's great with colors so she'll plan the color schemes and the football team and I will paint houses. Mike's going to broadcast the news on the school radio station. Bella will be the official greeter. She'll go from house to house to set up appointments.

NED

I've got space on my computer now to design posters. Deleted all the facts I didn't need.

MR. ABLE

And I've got time to help on construction if my little niece here will calculate percentages. Augusta,you'll be an important part of the group and we'll value your input. Will you do that?

AUGUSTA

Oh, yes, please! I'd love to.

PREZ

And Freddie. We'd like you to lend us something really special.

FREDDIE

What's that? I don't have anything really special.

PREZ

Oh, yes, you do. You're always eager and ready for new things, so we'd like to borrow your name. "The Ready Freddie Projects."

FREDDIE
Wow! Ready Freddie. Can we start soon?

PREZ
Sure thing. We'll begin next week. I'll
drive the bus again!

They all stare at him.

T.D.
Um, ah....we'll all take different vehicles.

PREZ
Oh! No bus?

ALL
No bus!!

PREZ
Okay, that's fine. I never did have a good
sense of direction anyway.

MIKE
Right!

T.D.
It's time to give Mr. Goodman his gift.

FREDDIE
This is a fun gift but we couldn't wrap it
up. Tell him, Angela.

ANGELA
Well, we identified with the numbers
just like you said and then we felt the
principle of numbers was taking care
of us kinda like a father and a mother.
So we're not worried about math or life
anymore. I composed a song about it. To
our dear teacher with love and respect, a
musical gift.

All students are present with teacher, and Mr. Able and Augusta to the side
watching also. The song can be choreographed to make it more interesting.

"CAROUSEL SONG" Version of 10's song

(Gals begin)
I had questions on perfection
It was chalk, or so I thought.
But it's the basis from which we figure
It's a fact and that is that.

So. . .

What can be done to better me?
Does the law of perfection apply?
What can be done to better me?
A number so perfect as I.

How can more beauty be given me?
New descriptions I simply defy.
How can more beauty be given me,
A number so lovely as I?

Our Mother loves us, tenderly loves us,
You're so dear and she is near.

(Guys sing)
Our Father guards us, watches o'er us,
Truth shines bright, we're in that light.

In that case. . .

What more light can be shone on me?
As an answer I hear a big sigh.
What more light can be shone on me?
A number so brilliant as I?

How could you be more pleased with me?
I know you'll just simply deny.
How could you be more pleased with me.
A number so faithful as I?

(Gals and Guys)
I had questions, endless questions.
Who am I and what am I?
Now my questions all have answers,
It's all true and yes for you.

They point to audience at that last line. During last verse Serena (Number 100) goes over to Mr. Able to ask him to dance by holding out her hand and the Kid (Number 5) goes to little helper, Augusta, bows to her, and she curtsies back to him and dances with him. Now six couples are waltzing, singing to next verse, as teacher watches.

(All)
What can be done to better me?
Does the law of perfection apply?
What can be done to better me,
A number so perfect as I?

They all waltz as they sing last verse of song and also waltz to the next verse which is without lyrics. This is the finale. They all hug and then take bows.

Cast takes group bows by singing a new verse to the audience, with arms outstretched. This is 10's tune but not waltz rhythm. 531 and 532 have the percent sign in the middle, holding its hands. They bow first.

As we work out from Principle
To know and to really see
As we work out from Principle
LOOK!
They exclaim this as music pauses, with arms toward audience.
There are numbers as perfect as we.

Repeat until all numbers take their bows. Then 10 sings alone to the music of "It's a matter of perfection." There is a musical track but bows could also be sung a Capella.

10

It's a needed liberation
And the truth that sets us free
Is that every single number
Is as perfect as can be.

She repeats the last line of melody with these words:

A perfect you and me.

She motions to audience, arms wide, palms of hands upwards then drops to a curtsy with arms out to the side, then palms of hands downwards as she sings "me." The players behind her join in this last line with bows and curtsies.

For our paths have come together now,
where do we go from here?

Will our differences divide us,
must we always live in fear?

For there are things that we must move through,
some things to cast aside.

While our Father watches over us,
our Mother will provide.

From the song, "It Amazes Me" by John Denver

Discussion points

Are we helped by placing this whole idea of a principle to life and our better selves in mathematical terms? Why?

Is the distinction between Numberland and Chalkland helpful to us in our own everyday life? If "yes" then how?

How is the love they talk about different from romantic love?

What can we take away from this play and workshop?

PROP LIST

Preplay scene
Lectern for teacher and ten chairs for pupils
Some background decoration with numerals and geometry signs.

Act 1   Off-stage.

Ball (large and same color as 5 is; must have bounce to it) for Number 5.
Football (same color as he is, paint it if necessary) for 39.
Microphone for Number 9.
Idealized briefcase (fairy-tale feel, same color as she) for Number 342, plus
wristwatch.
2 small flags (same color as 531) for 532 to wave, also pencil and pad tied to
her waist.
Hand mirror (color of 10) for Number 10.
Lectern set to side of stage to simulate Number 1's classroom, chairs to the
side.
4 large placards to be carried on stage. (On one side they all have a question
mark, ? And the other side 3 of them have 10 on them and one has 9.9)
Clipboard and pencil for Number 9, used again later by 911 and by 100.
Costume for percent sign.

On-stage.
Pinata or a cutout.
Percent sign on wall in preplay scene and final scene in real classroom.
Pinatas or cut-out numbers and geometry signs can be stage decoration.
Hat tree marked 911 with 7 hats (policeman, cowboy, mortar board, hard
hat plus 3 others).
Plants for 5 to sit near to be poured water on.
Waste-paper basket with a minus sign on it.
Watering can with water (?) for 10 to pour over 5.

Classroom scenes. On-stage.
Lectern for Number 1 with papers on it, (used later by 911 in Scene 5) and 10
chairs for pupils (more if larger cast is used).

Act 11, Scene 1, page 41 and 42   Off-stage.
Sheet music for 5 to carry on.
Minus signs made of cardboard or styrofoam.
Costume for zero.

Act 11, Scene 3
Students bring in either a maypole or a rendition of a colorful carousel.

Suggested set-up for classroom scene.

Lectern for teacher could be in the middle of the chairs and he and the class are all facing the audience and in a chevron shape. The main characters are on either side of him. If there is a larger cast the size of the class can be doubled with an extra row of chairs behind main characters. Also for larger cast, at end of mirror song, before 10 drops mirror in trash, many numbers could rush across the stage at back of her to the Rush Song. 10 looks at them and then drops mirror.

COSTUMING AND COLORS

Costuming: When in Chalkland, each player is dressed in one color entirely and so will be considered to be that color chalk. Color is determined by dress, not by skin. Their dress reflects their own concept of themselves. Perfect 10 could be in a long red dress with sash as winner of beauty pageant. See color chart below.

Odd numbers (males) should be distinctly different in their dress from evens (females).
Costumes for "real time" scenes are just current clothing, casual, but fitting the character. Final scene will have a party feel, so perhaps add wide skirts for girls for the dance.

PLEASE NOTE:
It is important to maintain the innocence of the whole piece in order for the ideas and idealism of the allegory to shine through. In order to do this, it is understood that any company performing this play agrees with this concept and will not dress players in seductive attire or use inappropriate language. And, though the play may lack worldly sophistication, it is definitely not juvenile. It will appeal, as do the CDs and the book, *Numberland,* to many people of all ages and cultures.

Suggested colors for numbers:

* These colors must be assigned as they appear in script.

411- narrator- turquoise or black
1- navy blue
100- pink*
911- orange
10-red*
39-green
Percent sign-white

5- yellow
33112- blue, washed out*
9-grey*
342- purple
531-brown
532-violet*

Life Adds Up in Numberland the Musical is available on Amazon.com. For *Numberland Songs as downloads or CDs please* fill out the contact form on the publisher's website:

www.MountaintopPublishing.com

www.ingramcontent.com/pod-product-compliance
Lightning Source LLC
Chambersburg PA
CBHW081542040426
42448CB00015B/3189